INTERVENTIONS
IN HISTORIC CENTRES

JC BUCKLER, SKETCH OF GENERAL VIEW OF MAGDALEN COLLEGE FROM THE SOUTH EAST

Architectural Design

INTERVENTIONS
IN HISTORIC CENTRES
THE BUILDING S OF MAGDALEN COLLEGE, OXFORD

OPPOSITE: THE CHAPEL, MAGDALEN COLLEGE, OXFORD; *ABOVE*: JC BUCKLER, PROPOSAL SKETCH FOR THE NEW BUILDING, MAGDALEN COLLEGE, OXFORD, 1820-21

ACADEMY EDITIONS • LONDON

Acknowledgements

All material is courtesy of the architects unless otherwise stated.
The basis for this magazine was the occasion of the International Forum on 'Interventions in Historic Centres'; held at Magdalen College, Oxford, on Saturday 17 October, 1992. This event was instigated and organised by Andreas Papadakis and sponsored by the Academy Group Ltd and Magdalen College, Oxford; chaired by Joseph Mordaunt Crook FBA of Royal Holloway, University of London and Dr Brian Hanson, Director of Studies, The Prince of Wales Institute of Architecture.
p46 Drawings by Joseph Altuna

Front Cover: *Demetri Porphyrios Associates, south elevation of Quadrangle, Magdalen College, Oxford;*
Back Cover: *Perspective view of Quadrangle, Magdalen College, Oxford;*
Inside Front and Back Covers: *Bodley and Garner, elevation facing the High Street and South side of Quadrangle, winning entry for the Magdalen Hall site competition, 1879*

Photographic Credits

pp1, 3, 14-35, Inside Front and Back Covers: Mario Bettella; *pp2, 12, 36-37, Back Cover:* John Gregg

CONSULTANTS: Catherine Cooke, Terry Farrell, Kenneth Frampton, Charles Jencks Heinrich Klotz, Leon Krier, Robert Maxwell, Demetri Porphyrios, Kenneth Powell, Colin Rowe, Derek Walker

HOUSE EDITOR: Maggie Toy GUEST EDITOR: Richard Economakis EDITORIAL TEAM: Nicola Hodges, Philippa Vice, Rachel Bean SENIOR DESIGNER: Andrea Bettella DESIGN CO-ORDINATOR: Mario Bettella DESIGN TEAM: Jason Rigby, Gregory Mills SUBSCRIPTIONS MANAGER: Mira Joka

First published in Great Britain in 1993 by *Architectural Design* an imprint of
ACADEMY GROUP LTD, 42 LEINSTER GARDENS, LONDON W2 3AN
ERNST & SOHN, HOHENZOLLERNDAMM 170, D-1000 BERLIN 31
Members of the VCH Publishing Group
ISBN: 1-85490-199-0 (UK)

Distributed in the United States of America by
ST MARTIN'S PRESS, 175 FIFTH AVENUE, NEW YORK, NY 10010

Printed and bound in Singapore

Contents

ARCHITECTURAL DESIGN PROFILE

INTERVENTIONS IN HISTORIC CENTRES

INTERVENTIONS FOR THE FUTURE

The question of how to build in historic city centres has increasingly troubled – and inspired – the architectural profession over the last 20 years. Stigmatised by the effects of five decades of modernist planning yet equipped with a fresh understanding and appreciation of tradition, architecture has reached what is arguably the most critical crossroads of the century.

Whether prompted by the strength of the pluralist argument or a more profound disaffection with the irreverence of high-tech consumer culture, architects around the world have begun to break out of the long period of self-imposed abstinence from contextual considerations, seeking ways by which to engage traditional and historic settings in meaningful dialogue and producing some of the most engaging proposals in recent times.

The emergence of a new critical movement founded in tradition and respectful of the forces of cultural continuity, so vigorously resisted by the Modern Movement, is clearly more a manifestation of outrage with the declining quality of contemporary urban space than an outpouring of nostalgic feeling that critics would have it be. Indeed, the greatest danger to this movement would be a wilful lapsing into mere stylistic considerations and loosening of the social, urban and tectonic arguments, as they have been expounded by theorists Leon Krier, Demetri Porphyrios and Maurice Culot, that have given it not just validity but a sense of urgency.

Despite the clarity of their message, however, differences abound amongst the new traditionalists, and raise questions concerning the exact nature of interventions. How far should historical precedents be taken as models? How are contemporary social and technological parameters incorporated in the new proposals? How should tradition and originality be understood? How can we retain traditional urban forms within the constraints of contemporary practice? What is the nature of the dialogue between architects and the people for whom they build?

At the heart of these questions is humanity's evolving relationship with the past, which involves the delicate issue of defining the terms 'historical' and 'modern'. The new traditionalists are almost unanimous in their view of the historical process – which in their way of thinking is not linear, as 'evolutionary' modernism maintains, but multi-dimensional. Life is not seen as an additive accumulation of phases or a constantly changing plot, but a recurrent reality, a play in which the actors and stage set may vary but which contains immutable truths and conditions. A street, according to this view, *requires* definition; a city *needs* the dialogue between public and private space; adjacent buildings *ought* to respect each other, both aesthetically and formally; true invention is not obsessive and seeks only to solve *inherent* (as opposed to construed) problems; modernity is not irreverent but *respectful* and in debt to the past.

It is more important, argue the new traditionalists, to seek common ground than it is to bring out the differences, though these must be honoured.

It was precisely for this reason – the search for common ground – that the International Forum on 'Interventions in Historic Centres' was held at Magdalen College, Oxford, on Saturday 17 October, 1992. Organised concurrently with a presentation of Demetri Porphyrios' winning proposal for the new Longwall Quadrangle, the event brought together some of the world's foremost theorists, historians and practitioners, including Rob Krier, Terry Farrell, Demetri Porphyrios, John Simpson, Maurice Culot, David Watkin and Oswyn Murray. The symposium, chaired by Dr Brian Hanson of The Prince of Wales Institute of Architecture and Joseph Mordaunt Crook of Royal Holloway, University of London, was opened with a poignant talk by the President of Magdalen College, Anthony Smith, followed by a survey of the history of interventions at Magdalen College by Roger White.

This issue puts together the proceeds of the event, recorded in the excerpts from the forum transcripts, and focuses on specific projects as case studies for the problem of interventions.

Richard Economakis

OPPOSITE: Magdalen College, Oxford

7

ANTHONY SMITH

INTERVENTIONS AT MAGDALEN COLLEGE, OXFORD

Speech given by Anthony Smith, President of Magdalen College, on the occasion of the International Forum on 'Interventions in Historic Centres'; held at Magdalen College, Oxford, on Saturday 17 October, 1992.

Let me begin by pointing out that Magdalen's very existence was itself an intervention in the urban landscape of Oxford brought on by the requirements of social and ideological change. Magdalen Hall was already established in crowded premises in the High Street early in the 15th century when William of Waynflete conceived the idea of taking over the hospital and almshouse of St John and converting it to a college dedicated to the New Learning of Bacon and his followers. One institution replaced the other, at first in terms of use and then, more gradually, in its buildings until very little of the former institution remained. The real pressure for change came from the process of the transformation of learning and of the role of the University in the life of society.

The ensemble of buildings we possess today is the result of five centuries of fevered and furious arguments, of frequent demolitions and replacements, each new generation left to face new and more intense controversies when further development became necessary. In the 1990s we are again experiencing changes in the urban environment which also affect the nature of academic life; and these changes have resulted in the new quadrangle project at Magdalen which forms the starting point for our meeting today.

For well over a decade the routes of the A40 and the M40 have constituted a private avenue from Marble Arch to Oxford, which has come gradually to become part of the commuting hinterland of London. Now that the link with Birmingham has been created, Birmingham is also within commuting distance. The housing market of Oxford has merged with that of London. Oxford's rather pleasant environment means that the needs of its universities and industries are not the only shaping forces of its housing market. Since the late 1960s the number of students and resident academics has continued to grow and dozens of private commercial schools and academic establishments have moved into the area. Pressure on housing for students of all kinds has grown more intense. The city attempted to regulate the situation by coming to an agreement with the University to the effect that it would never allow its numbers to grow in such a manner as to have more than 4,000 students on the local housing market. That agreement was to run until roughly now and it was a good way of coping with an ever-changing and essentially uncontrollable situation.

But now the shaping factors are well outside the region of Oxford itself. The housing market of Oxford has changed radically. There were once streets and streets of privately owned student digs but these houses have been acquired by small rack-renting companies, brandishing 11-month tenancies at 50 or more pounds per week, grasping and merciless, as motherly as a banking machine.

We can no longer leave students at the mercy of this market, for it is changing the nature of university life in very damaging ways. We have preserved virtually intact a unique and enviable tutorial system, which depends not upon modules of learning but continuous residence in close proximity with teachers. Students are now paying more in rent than their entire official income. We do not want them to take jobs during the academic year. They are part of a college community and they should be able to live within it throughout their time here. Many of them today are unable to feed themselves adequately because of the ludicrous cost of housing. The most urgent form of subsidy which we feel it is appropriate to offer them is full housing for the three or four years they spend here. That applies to both graduates and undergraduates.

To house the whole student population has become Oxford's quest of the era. Some colleges are building cheap student hostels. Magdalen, however, has been provided by history with the great blessing of a very large estate, of river walks and formal and informal gardens as well as several private tracts of half-cultivated river banks and an orchard, seldom seen by the public. We have held on to every inch of our land for over half a millennium. It seemed natural, therefore, for us to try to build within the 15th-century walls and to do so on a scale which would last as far ahead as we can see. We have no plan to expand our student numbers but we do want to be able to say to every single student: if you want to live within the college you can.

We could not decide, at first, where in our large estate we should try to build, but we fixed on two sites; the first is called Holywell Ford, an arts-and-crafts movement family house, said to be the origin of the house in *Wind in the Willows*. It is also where Dylan Thomas is said to have written *Under Milk Wood*. There were various ways in which a building could be placed here, but all of them would undoubtedly transform the lost-world atmosphere which envelops that old house.

The second site is that currently occupied by the fellows' car park and our old and ugly squash courts, just inside Longwall Gate. This is in no sense a lost rural environment, it is close to the heart of the college and there would be great visual benefit in placing the car park underground. The site is a sensitive one. We decided to ask a number of selected architects to advise us which site to use. In the event they all said it would be a shame to build more than a limited amount of accommodation at Holywell Ford, even though the area is officially designated for future academic use. Some of them produced schemes, one or two refused even to do so.

The process of choosing an architect and a policy took about a year in all. First we made a list of about 14 architects, some of them firms who had worked for us in the recent past when we were engaged in a vast project of restoration and conservation, now happily concluded. Some were personal choices based on buildings we had seen and liked. One or two were volunteers who had heard about the project on the grapevine.

It was clear that there was going to be serious and perhaps long debate and that any design we chose would be controversial, but in the event our plan of systematic and wide consultation brought us to a clear decision. In the first stage all 14 architects were asked to visit the site. The Senior Bursar and I then set aside half a day for each to be briefed about the nature of the college and the background to the project. We gave them all printed material about the college and a brief setting out the reasons for our needing to build and the amount of accommodation we hoped to achieve. They all responded and gave us their time, but one or two dropped out almost immediately because they did not wish to go to the trouble and expense of preparing even a first-stage plan, when the competitors were still rather numerous.

We were, and are, highly ambitious. We want the building to be of the highest standard possible and to last for generations. We do not want anything of which we might be ashamed in 20 or 30 years time. Not another Waynflete Building, everyone warned us.

The 12 remaining architects produced a variety of designs, rough draughts or simply manifestos and these were whittled down to six. Our search committee of seven Fellows went to visit a building designed by each of them and discussed their work on site. The number was then reduced to three. The short-listed architects were asked to make presentations at some length to the whole of the Fellowship; for it is only the whole Fellowship which can make a decision of this importance.

Meanwhile the designs for the Longwall site were being exhibited at College meetings and in our Common Room. They were shown to our Development Trust and the students were encouraged to examine the designs and to hold meetings to discuss the final short list. Both the Junior and Middle Common Rooms held meetings and debated the two surviving schemes. They came out overwhelmingly in favour of the Porphyrios design. It seemed to me that a number of my colleagues, perhaps somewhat torn by the decision between two radically different approaches, were influenced by the strength of the student preference.

The preference for the Porphyrios scheme clearly had much to do with the fact that it took full cognisance of the nature of the Oxford quadrangle and the Oxford staircase. The latter is treated not only as a means for reaching a room; it is a psychologically important space, guarding privacy and creating a social unit. Some of the participating architects did not really grasp the subtle social nature of the Oxford staircase. Given a quadrangle rather than a single block or an L-shaped building and given the staircase formula, the rest of the Porphyrios design followed. The

rival designs offered imaginative, modernistic approaches but simply did not develop the ensemble of our buildings in a way which we would recognise as 'home' in Oxford terms.

We saw in the Porphyrios design the continuity of a residential tradition, and we opted for that continuity not out of mere conservativism, but because it was the inevitable consequence of the original brief. Our existing ensemble of buildings is so deeply inscribed in the memory of Oxford people, that I do not believe we would ultimately have constructed any of the other schemes, even if the Porphyrios design had not been on offer. That is of course an entirely personal view.

The chosen design uses elements of the Magdalen vernacular, as Porphyrios calls it, to weave a variety of buildings into a setting for the commanding presence of the classical lecture theatre and recital room. I was fascinated to discover in the course of my conversations with one of the other architects, one whom I found attractive in approach, that his design was slowly evolving over the months of discussion towards similar 'Magdalen vernacular'; he was beginning to notice and adopt features drawn from the existing library of buildings. It began to dawn on me that given enough time, many of the competing architects might slowly come round to the same ideas to which Demetri Porphyrios had gone directly. As the rival designs evolved they might perhaps have ended up with an open quadrangle holding a group of staircases together. There is something very beguiling about Magdalen's quadrangles: three sides of buildings and the fourth open to views across our walks and parks.

What Demetri Porphyrios Associates achieved was to complete this intellectual and design journey in one go and in my view this project reaches the destination in a glorious sweep. It gives us a collection of buildings forming an asymmetric quadrangle, open to the Deer Park and with views on to the classical New Buildings which will always remain Magdalen's ultimate *coup de theatre*; Porphyrios has not attempted to upstage New Buildings, but rather to support their performance with a kind of *entr'acte*. He provides nearly 100 students and tutors with rooms and sets of rooms with their own bathrooms, in a small group of buildings. He has noticed that we have towers starting in Longwall Street and culminating in Wolsey's Great Tower and he has continued the sequence, so that a giant standing over us will see a progression of towers from the corner of Holywell Street to Magdalen Bridge. He has also hidden a car park beneath the new lawn and, as a bonus, a number of other public rooms for seminars, offices and storage which we badly need but thought we could not achieve.

Our students continue to love the design, as do some of our recent benefactors. Old members of the College offer their allegiance to it, some with relief, others with enthusiasm. We have hardly, however, begun to tackle the problem of funding. That, in this present financial climate, may take a little time. I do hope that what I have said provides a useful case history in the development of a project which intervenes in an ancient urban landscape, treating surrounding streets with respect, while pointing up the felicities of its immediate environment and succeeding, in my view, to be beautiful.

ACADEMY INTERNATIONAL FORUM
INTERVENTIONS IN HISTORIC CENTRES
Extracts from the Discussion

Brian Hanson: Joe Mordaunt Crook and I would like to welcome you to our symposium. We have heard from President Smith the history behind the selection of Demetri Porphyrios' scheme for the New Longwall Quadrangle. Let's take a moment and discuss generally the situation of Magdalen historically and currently. Could I ask the President first: did you consider finishing off the New Buildings as an alternative?

Anthony Smith: Yes, we did. There is no discussion ever about building in which someone does not ask: 'Why don't we just go back and improve or extend what we already have'. I think that we would have had 3,000 or so old members lying down in front of the bulldozers before the commencement of works. A lot has been said about the character of Magdalen's architectural planning, but I feel that perhaps it would help to put it into historical context. The standard type of Oxford college is a closed quadrangle which goes back to the Middle Ages, but there are a few colleges which have large gardens that spill into the grounds. In the course of time, Magdalen developed a system of interconnected courts. The peculiar character of Magdalen might be said to be the layering of the plan, which is the accidental result of building over the years.

Demetri Porphyrios: I'm not really sure what strategies were chosen by the other architects involved in the initial phases of the design selection, but we took the time to go through the archives of the college and understand its history. It is clear to me that a substantial amount of 'accident' accounts for what is generally considered to be a beautiful or picturesque composition. I was aware of this before we started working on the project in the office; we had to decide whether we should formalise the quadrangle or leave it open to the deer park.

Ken Powell: Were you in any anguish about responding to the local vernacular vocabulary here, and did you come to your present solution after a process which perhaps began with a more Classical tradition with which you have been associated?

Demetri Porphyrios: No, there was no such agonising over the local vernacular. It did take some time, involving discussions with members of the design team, particularly Nigel Cox and Alireza Sagharchi, before we put pen to paper. I sense no conflict, however, when considering what Classical, Gothic or vernacular architecture are. There is a hierarchy of buildings beginning with the vernacular, which is straightforward building; all the way to the highest form of load-bearing architecture, which is the Classical. Between those two extremes all forms of load-bearing vocabularies can take place. As regards the Magdalen context, a substantial number of buildings are straightforward, 'bread-and-butter' housing blocks, and as such they represent a local vernacular typology, the sort which constitutes the basic fabric of cities. We decided, furthermore, to extract from the brief an important feature, namely the auditorium, and give it a special honorific presence.

Ken Powell: Can I ask you about the 'Magdalen Vernacular', How do you propose to make your buildings convincingly vernacular in

an age when craftsmanship has been defunct? I am worried about where the dividing line comes between decorum and propriety.

Demetri Porphyrios: There are two parts in your question. One raises the issue of whether 'Magdalen vernacular' is a proper term to use. The other throws doubt on whether anything that demands good craftsmanship is at all possible today. As regards the first point, I should say that vernacular provides a minimal symbolic transition from construction to stylised form. When you construct something in a straightforward manner, without a specific emphasis on symbolism, one produces basic, simple building, and in that sense one constructs in a vernacular way. The second part of your question is important because if one assumes that today it is not possible to build solidly, then obviously not much of substance can, in fact, be built. Yet I do believe strongly that not only can buildings be solidly built today, but that the trends of industrial production will change to such an extent that we shall see substantially increased examples of this traditional construction.

John Simpson: I don't see why Demetri should have any problems in realising his proposal for Magdalen. Certainly my experience of building has shown me that there is no real shortage of crafts, or shortage of skills. We may not have as many craftsmen as were available, say, in the late 19th century, but the skills are still there.

John Brandon Jones: The only secret of success for architects as modern craftsmen is that you must know enough about craftsmanship to be able to answer the right thing and to be able to say 'No, that is not good enough'. When I was building the Hampshire County Offices in 1958-60, I said to my client 'I suppose that's all we can expect nowadays'. He said to me, 'Mr Voysey would have had it down'. I replied, 'Oh, you think they can do better than that; all right, take it down and do it again'. And they did beautiful brickwork on that job.

Keith Wills: May I add to that, speaking on behalf of Magdalen College. I think we do owe a lot to Brandon Jones for his advice on the College restoration and his contribution in supervising the works. The restoration of the tower itself is indeed very beautiful.

Terry Farrell: I think that the most interesting aspect in Demetri's presentation, if one reads his 'intervention' not just at the level of architectural vocabulary but as a piece of town-planning, is that it is legible as being a group of residences dedicated to one type of occupant. It is a collective, yet at the same time it is a part, being, as it is, tucked behind a wall. The wall itself goes round several quadrangles at Magdalen in which there are similar buildings, so it is a typology that repeats within the college. Yet it is a piece of its own because it has its own master building, its own central or community building, namely the auditorium. It contributes positively to the very unique nature of the town of Oxford.

Philip Dowson: Taking a parallel academic building by Giancarlo de Carlo in Urbino where that particular intervention is enormously successful, it is important to note that there the new building retains a distance from the roots that surround it. It is stunningly beautiful and, from talking to students, it appears that they see a kind of building which manifests notions of hope, for it actually looks forward in a very particular way.

Robert Adam: I want to respond to something that Ken Powell said earlier which cut a particular cord with me because I was one of the invited architects for Magdalen that did not get to be one of the finalists. Perhaps one of the reasons is that I had reached a similar conclusion to the one you, Kenneth, have expressed about Gothic Revival: namely that it had run out by the time Scott got to it and that really this is over, ended and should not be picked up at all. What I find interesting is that Demetri is not producing an idea of Gothic as being something essentially English or Catholic Revival. I think it is a mistake just to look at the pieces and say, 'Ah, yes, this is the same thing as Scott was doing but just the tail end of it'. An entirely different ethos of solid vernacular buildings is produced here. We are now dealing with something new and different.

Rob Krier: The discussion we had earlier about style, about Gothic or Classical or vernacular vocabularies, is not really our problem today. I personally do not feel that the quality of craftsmanship today is in any way comparable to what we know existed up to the late 19th century. The same criticism applies to the quality of architectural thinking and urban composition. That is our desperation as modern designers. At Amiens we made a proposal which would involve numerous architects, and encouraged them to think freely but always along the simple lines characteristic of buildings that make up the basic, traditional urban fabric. In doing so we are not involving ourselves with the question of style and ornament, but we focus on the urban repertoire.

William Whitfield: One interesting point that has emerged is to do with the way we see buildings, especially public buildings. People at large tend to think that the more you can see of architecture in one sweep of the eye, the better. This is wrong. If we compare the situation of St Peter's in Rome with that of the Duomo in Florence, we realise the very important difference: in Florence you discover the cathedral a little bit at a time as you move down the streets. Every time you see it you feel it is your own personal discovery, not something that somebody else has devised for you. To me this is enormously important because it means that there is a personal involvement with the way you appreciate buildings and I argue that you do not have to see a public building full frontal all in one piece. It so happens that at the moment I am designing the building which will replace the existing Juxon House next to St Paul's. The only way to get the good view of St Paul's again is to bring back the original building line. I do believe that in some way we must help people understand that the unfolding cityscape, the juxtaposition of what I call a community of buildings to their great neighbour the cathedral, is something that is not as simple as merely a boulevard with a monument at the end of it. That is a different order of things which has its own interest but it does not provide you with that sense of personal discovery. The other point I want to make refers to the difficulties we face when dealing with very sensitive historical environments. Today new building techniques remove the 'hands', as it were, from the facades of buildings. Such buildings do not sit well, by and large, in historic areas. There is a need to build new buildings that have something extra which gives them the complexity of texture that is available with buildings built by hands, rather than with pre-fabricated lumps.

Philip Dowson: I think we are going over rather well-known ground. The case for contextualism has been made. But I don't think we are addressing a very fundamental issue, namely that cities change; they flourish and they decline. Le Corbusier said,'let's pull it all down, let's have roads running through it, let's create a new city'. We tried this and we have now returned to the traditional city, the corridor city, but we still have not solved the issue that Le Corbusier raised, how do you deal with this new kind of city where instead of being just a small built-up area, it is a great metropolis. I don't think this issue has even been raised this afternoon.

John Simpson: We have destroyed our cities so much that people get to the point where they feel that enough destruction is enough, and they prefer to see something that is more positive in terms of reconstruction. I think that people are more interested in achieving a recognisable sense of grace, something which is not abstract, something that they can relate to in terms of tradition.

Maurice Culot: In our project for the rue de Laeken in Brussels we enjoyed contemplating the question of style, and like a ghost ship we drifted from revolution to counter-revolution. I no longer feel the desire to change the world, not even a small bit. Though I am still fond of originality, I must say that I have come to dislike militancy. I look for what I like, for what is close to my true sensibility. I enjoy the process of imitation, I am not afraid of the word *decorum*. I look for what is pleasing. Looking around me in my travels I see that the quality of public space has deteriorated vastly, except in the centres of towns. We must think of our public spaces again as a stage-set for the unfolding drama of our lives, and give it the qualities we truly cherish and aspire to.

Brian Hanson: A lot of what we've heard today demonstrates a consensus on a particular point of view about building in historic centres: it should be contextual, it should possess a vitality which perhaps modernist language and the modernist process of construction denies. One thing that is also noteworthy is that today the discussion of style is increasingly (and mercifully) absent and that one is beginning to talk about more fundamental issues like the planning and urban implications of interventions. Style did rear its head in this forum but wonderfully, as something to be enjoyed and experienced on a very sensual level. Another point that came out of this event is that historical knowledge, looking carefully at old plans, studying the context of a site, is indispensable. Demetri has shown us the quality that can be brought out of a brief at the moment when one fuses the knowledge of a place's history and the love of the place. Perhaps in this there are seeds for future debates.

FORUM PARTICIPANTS

Robert Adam, *Architect;* Clive Aslet, *Country Life;* John Barron, *St Peter's College;* Nancy Bell, *Magdalen College;* Julian Bicknell, *Architect;* John Brandon Jones, *Architectural Historian;* Edward Chaney, *English Heritage;* Howard Colvin, *St John's College;* Janie Cottis, *Magdalen College;* Nigel Cox, *Architect;* J Mordaunt Crook, *Professor of Architectural History, London;* Dan Cruickshank, *Architects Journal;* Maurice Culot, *Architectural Critic;* Sheila de Vallee, *Academy Group;* Philip Dowson, *Architect;* Richard Economakis, *Architect;* Terry Farrell, *Architect;* Paul Finch, *Building Design;* Brian Hanson, *The Prince of Wales's Institute;* Richard John, *Merton College;* Rob Krier, *Architect;* Andreas Papadakis, *Academy Group;* Demetri Porphyrios, *Architect;* Kenneth Powell, *Daily Telegraph;* Bernard Richards, *Oxford Architectural Society;* Alireza Sagharchi, *Architect;* Edwina Sassoon, *Art Consultant;* John Simpson, *Architect;* Anthony Smith, *Magdalen College;* Madeleine von Heland, *National Museum, Stockholm;* David Watkin, *Peterhouse College, Cambridge;* Roger White, *Architectural Historian;* William Whitfield, *Architect;* Keith Wills, *Magdalen College;* Giles Worsley, *Country Life*

JOSEPH MORDAUNT CROOK
GOOD AND BAD MANNERS IN ARCHITECTURE

I suspect that one of the themes about which we shall be hearing a considerable amount today is the theme of architectural manners, good and bad. When Andreas Papadakis invited me to chair this opening session, I made it my business to find out who was the first architectural theorist to talk of *politeness* in architecture. I think it was Edward Lacy Garbett in his *Principles of Design in Architecture* (1850; 1863). He makes politeness not only one characteristic of architecture, but *the* characteristic. What exactly did he mean? He certainly did not mean a prissy self-effacement, or any lack of visual expression. He meant that no building can exist in a vacuum, as a kind of functional hypothesis: it has to be seen, as well as used; and seen by many more people who do not own it than by those who do. Once built, any building has multiple consequences – visually, socially, imagistically. Merely by existing, a building engages in that reciprocal process (design + perception = image), that dialogue of creation and judgement which we try to explain under the general heading of aesthetics. If it doesn't; if it declines to engage in dialogue; if it tries to exist merely *of itself*, it is manifestly selfish. It is not spectator-friendly. It says to the world, in the im-

mortal words of Owen Luda, PPRIBA: 'Sod you!' Let me quote Mr Garbett:

> What makes a building 'unarchitectural . . . is . . . I believe this quality of *selfishness*'. 'I am quite prepared to be laughed at', he says, 'and told that . . . this is a mental quality . . . nothing . . . to do with bricks or stones . . . On the contrary . . . it is not the building we admire or condemn, but the mind that appears in it . . . A building devoid of architecture displeases all who see it . . . because it benefits its owner at their expense – they have not been thought of in the design . . . (it doesn't care) that there are eyes without as well as within. It is this crude selfish *rudeness* which requires to be softened down by *politeness* . . . and this politeness we term Architecture . . . Goethe (may have) called Gothic architecture 'petrified religion' . . . (I call) domestic architecture . . . embodied courtesy.

There it is, the case for contextuality. I wonder if anybody will put it better than that today? If we are to put that argument better – more humanely, more poetically – we need to bear in mind the dying words of William Morris: 'I want to get mumbo-jumbo out of the world'. That might even do as our motto.

OPPOSITE: Magdalen College, Oxford; LEFT: JC Buckler, design for south gateway to Magdalen College, 1820-21

To the Reverend Dr ROUTH, PRESIDENT, and the FELLOWS of SAINT MARY MAGDALEN COLLEGE, OXFORD. This Print representing the SOUTH EAST VIEW of MAGDALEN COLLEGE TOWER &c, is by Permission most humbly Dedicated by their much obliged and devoted Servant

14

ROGER WHITE

THE ARCHITECTURAL EVOLUTION OF MAGDALEN COLLEGE

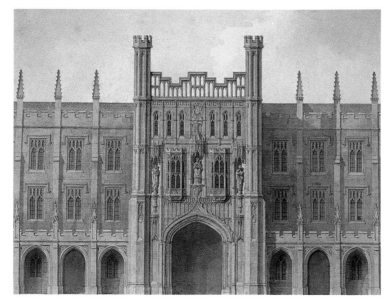

JC BUCKLER, PROPOSAL FOR GATEWAY, MAGDALEN COLLEGE, OXFORD, 1820-21

In *Unbuilt Oxford*, that magisterial survey of the architectural might-have-beens of a university city, Howard Colvin devotes a whole chapter to Magdalen College. He entitles it 'Indecision at Magdalen', and he characterises some two centuries of college history, from the 1720s to the 1920s, as 'an epic of architectural mismanagement'.[1] 'The result,' he concludes, 'is a collection of buildings that, despite the quality of their architecture and the beauty of their setting, still lacks the essential unity of a college'. By contrast, with this severe judgement Demetri Porphyrios, architect of the 1991 scheme to redevelop the site between Longwall Street and the deer park, has spoken of Magdalen's 'unique quadrangle organisation that is enclosed yet open . . . boundaries are soft, with open vistas (so that) a sense of both enclosure and perspectival freedom is achieved'.

Magdalen College, Oxford was founded by Bishop Waynflete of Winchester in 1458, and the buildings which form the original nucleus went up between 1473 and about 1510. The great bell tower (Fig 1) that supplies the most prominent feature of the ensemble was the final piece to be built (1492-1509), together with the flanking ranges along the High Street which incorporate relatively insignificant remnants of the preceding building on the site, St John's Hospital; also from the earlier buildings is the former kitchen east of the hall, which is said to be late 13th or early 14th century.

The remainder of Waynflete's foundation buildings, including chapel and hall, are set back from the street and arranged around a cloister – an arrangement which came to be seen as epitomising the late-medieval ideal of a quasi-monastic college, self-contained and inward-looking, even though it is found nowhere else at Oxford or Cambridge (the earlier cloister at New College encloses a burial ground and is non-residential, while the cloister walks intended at Christ Church were never built).[2] Since no documentation survives to elucidate the precise intentions of the Founder and his architects, we cannot know whether the lack of a formal axial relationship between cloister and tower betokens an afterthought, but it was to provide the formally-inclined architects of the first half of the 18th century with something of a headache.

Although the elements of seemingly casual asymmetry found in Waynflete's buildings are not in the least surprising in a late medieval context, the device of the cloister serves to provide an ordered focus and to emphasise the closed nature of the quadrangle form. It is this closed form which is depicted virtually unaltered by the passage of nearly two centuries in Loggan's bird's-eye view of 1675 (Fig 2) – and which remained to challenge the college authorities when major additions were first contemplated in the 1720s. Loggan also shows the two other main spaces of the college, each quite

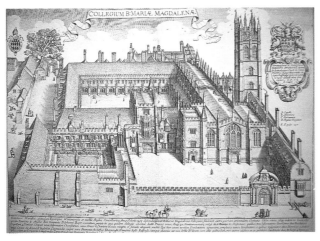

2

3

4

5

firmly enclosed: a subsidiary quadrangle enclosed by the library on the east, President's Lodgings on the south, the Election Gallery on the north; and what became St John's Quad, enclosed by buildings on three sides and a high embattled wall on the fourth. Into the otherwise homogeneously late-medieval Gothic of this ensemble intrude two classical notes which were to constitute a growing visual irritant in the 19th century, namely the grand baroque gate added as the college's main entrance around 1635, [3] and a lesser portal which framed the passage through to the cloister.

By the early 18th century most Oxford colleges were in expansive mood, for the cramped conditions that were the medieval norm (with fellows sharing rooms not only with other fellows but also with students) were no longer acceptable, especially given the growing trend for the nobility and landed gentry to send their sons to university. Some colleges, Magdalen among them, began by adopting the cheap and easy expedient of adding attics or 'cocklofts' to existing ranges (Fig 3) but then went on to plan new buildings which would cater particularly for the influx of gentleman commoners.[4] In this period Queens and Worcester were engaged in effectively rebuilding themselves, Christ Church, University and All Souls were expanding, and Magdalen and Brasenose were contemplating the prospect. In the case of Magdalen the rationale seems to have been a combination of actual need and perceived dilapidation (in 1720 Hearne was told that the fellows had 'unanimously agreed at Magdalen College . . . to pull down and rebuild the east side of that College'; and Hawksmoor was to express the view in 1724 that the fabric was so decrepit that there was little point in repairing anything except the hall and chapel, and that all ought to be rebuilt); but there is no doubt too that building and rebuilding were then very much in the Oxford air.

The ruthlessness of the approach to expansion which some fellows at least were prepared to countenance is indicated by a vignette in the Magdalen Benefactors Book (Fig 4), recording a benefaction made in 1720 by Dr Edward Butler (who was to be elected President two years later), specifically to start a building fund. The bell tower appears as the sole survivor of the Founder's work, its base opened up to form the main entrance of the college and set between elaborate wrought iron screens on the chord of a great crescent. As Howard Colvin points out, this may be no more than a calligrapher's fancy but it nevertheless seems to constitute the first known design for a residential crescent (predating the Royal Crescent in Bath by 47 years).

A scarcely less sweeping attitude is displayed in two sketch schemes from the same period. One of

The glass of the west window had been badly damaged by a storm in 1703 and never fully restored. In 1785 the college received a benefaction of £300 earmarked for a new west window. The fellows, however, preferred the idea of restoration, and in 1789 consulted Thomas Jervais, who had in 1778-85 executed Sir Joshua Reynolds' design for the west window of New College Chapel. To their disappointment Jervais not only concluded that repair was impracticable but declined to undertake the painting of a replacement. The college's first impulse was to spend the money on reglazing the remaining antechapel windows 'something like those of All Souls', but it may be that the benefactor disapproved, for the college next turned for advice to James Wyatt, then busy 'restoring' New College Chapel.

Wyatt recommended Francis Eginton, a fashionable glazier of Handsworth near Birmingham, whom the college contacted in 1791 and in 1793 commissioned to proceed with the 'repairs'. Eginton's technique is described by him in a letter of July 1794 to the then President, Dr Martin Routh:

I have repainted every part and instead of the cold tint which pervaded the whole of this and every other window I have seen in Claro oscuro, I have defus'd a general warm tint throughout, which gives harmony to the colours and will produce a soft and pleasant light in the chapel.

Barely 30 years later John Chessel Buckler was to write of Eginton's contribution:

the painted glass . . . is decidedly the worst in Oxford. Such is its general character, that it casts a feverish hue over the interior; and viewing the chapel from the Altar-steps, without the aid of a summer-evening's sun, it is difficult to imagine in what other way than by a bonfire in the Antechapel so gloomy and deeptoned a glare could be produced.[8]

So delighted were the fellows in 1795, however, that they commissioned Eginton to fill the eight smaller windows of the Antechapel with new glass to his designs. The subject matter, agreed by the college, included the college arms; John the Baptist and St Mary Magdalen; the Baptism and Entombment of Christ; and the episcopal founders of four colleges, Waynflete, Wykeham, Fox and Wolsey.

Meanwhile, in 1790, concern about the condition of the timber roofs of chapel and hall had prompted the college to consult Wyatt about more fundamental changes. Writing in 1823, JC Buckler (who presumably had the inside story from his father John, whose connection with Magdalen went back to 1785) recalled that a survey of the roofs was made by a local builder, 'and their condemnation of

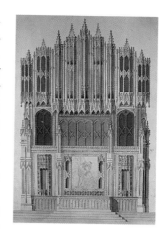

11

course followed'.[9] Even though the roofs had apparently been well maintained, Wyatt refused to guarantee their safety for another 24 hours. 'Necessity was pleaded, but fashion (for at the time of which I am speaking Mr Wyatt was in the zenith of his renown and was engaged in similar undertakings all over the kingdom) lurked behind and prompted the measure'. The roofs were consequently replaced, with plaster Gothic vaults set below the rafters, and in the chapel canopied niches were inserted between the windows (Fig 10). 'It was', commented Buckler, 'a principal fault of Mr Wyatt that, in 'Gothic' Architecture, he built more for show than real use'; he wanted Magdalen Chapel 'to exhibit . . . the meretricious splendour with which he loaded the interior of New College Chapel'.

Wyatt went on in 1792 to produce designs for completing the transformation of the chapel interior, proposing to de-classicise it by the installation of a new reredos (for which he offered three alternative designs (Fig 11), one of them based on that of Waynflete's chantry in Winchester Cathedral, and another rather spectacularly incorporating the organ pipes), panelling, choir stalls, screen and organ loft. His beguiling coloured drawings conceal the fact, revealed by the written estimates, that in addition to the use of carved wood and stone much of the work was to be of 'composition'. New College Chapel was the much-admired touchstone, and it is rather surprising that in the event his ideas were not proceeded with.

The reason is perhaps that with the installation in April 1791 of a new President, thoughts had begun to turn back to the unresolved matter of the new quadrangle. Dr Martin Routh, a distinguished theological scholar, was elected at the age of 35. By the age of 40 he was already being referred to as 'venerable', but he remained to head the college until his death in 1854 at the age of 99.[10] Although in general terms he exerted a deeply conservative influence, preferring to retain long-established customs even if they clearly departed from the intentions of the Founder's statutes,[11] in architectural matters he was often unexpectedly willing, even eager, to alter the status quo. Wyatt's changes to the chapel had been initiated before his election, but he evidently admired and promoted them. In his 1823 *Observations* Buckler was careful to credit Routh with deep knowledge of ecclesiastical architecture and with an almost saintly determination to apply the brake to ill-considered innovation, so as to transmit the college fabric 'venerable and uninjured to posterity'. In a more frank memoir written in 1858, he commented that:

it is a very singular fact that although the President would discourse from morn till night

12

VIEW of a NEW QUADRANGLE for MAGDALEN COLLEGE, OXFORD.

13

upon ancient architecture, he had no real regard for it. Wyatt's plans owe their origin to the President, who never faltered in his admiration of what that architect had done, and what he proposed to do.

At some point in 1791, presumably at Routh's prompting, Wyatt sent in his ideas for completing the Great Quadrangle. He worked on the assumption that ways had to be found of uniting the incomplete New Building to the medieval nucleus by the introduction of continuous ranges. Neither Hawksmoor, Clarke, Holdsworth nor Townesend had felt shy about the immediate juxtaposition of Gothic and classical, but by the 1790s, although the classical option remained, there was a growing feeling that the new work should defer stylistically to the old. Gothic – or Gothick – was already in the air at Magdalen, for preceding the proposals for the chapel came a charming new Gothick bog-house, known as West's Building [12] and built alongside the Cherwell in 1782 by John Burrough and Stephen Townesend. [13] In 1791 an elaborate Gothic throne was carved from an ancient and recently fallen oak tree, to the design of Richard Paget, a demy 'well skilled in antiquities'. A former Vice-President of the college, Dr Ambrose Kent, wrote to Routh in January 1792 that 'all Honour should be done to the Founder's original Plan; and the more any additions are assimilated to it, the greater credit will it reflect, in my opinion, upon the just Taste of the present members'.

Wyatt's plan (Fig 12) was that the New Building could be brought in from the cold, and a vista opened up from it south to the bell tower, by removing the intervening north side of the cloisters. Linking ranges in Wyatt's characteristic pared-down Tudor Gothic, punctuated on each side by replicas of the Founder's Tower, would enclose the much enlarged space thus created, but no suggestion was yet made of completing the assimilation by refronting the New Building in Gothic. The disparity in width between the old quadrangle and the new offered the possibility of inserting a new library at the northwest corner of the cloisters.

Routh's canvassing of Wyatt's scheme elicited several objections on the grounds of expense (which Wyatt in July 1792 calculated at £19,000), and for several years the matter rested. The President did however act on a suggestion of Dr Kent's, that Wyatt be asked to produce designs for 'an elegant Gothick Screen and Gateway' to replace the solid wall and classical portal that obstructed views of the chapel from the High Street. Wyatt obliged with several variants, none of which were taken up, but it was a subject to which other architects were to address themselves in the ensuing decades.

Discussion of grand designs was revived in 1795,

when Routh apparently suggested that Wyatt should think in terms of removing the old quadrangle altogether and, alternatively, of developing the site of Magdalen Hall. The architect, not surprisingly, liked the idea of dispensing with the 'extremely inconvenient' cloisters very much, but any proposals that may have resulted seem not to have survived. The following year the young John Buckler, clerk to the college Steward, sent in a pair of attractive perspectives (Fig 13) illustrating a classical variation on Wyatt's 1791 theme. Though at the end of his long life Buckler told Dr Bloxam that he had preferred sketching cathedrals and parish churches to building or repairing 'sash-windowed dwellings', [14] in consequence of which he had never tried to develop his career as an architect, he nevertheless on this occasion envisaged beefing up the New Building by the addition of an Ionic portico and framing it with a further pair of porticoed blocks; the component parts would have been linked to each other and to the medieval buildings by classical arcades. Buckler shows the north cloister range removed and replaced by a single-storey cloister in simple pointed Gothic. [15] It was a not unattractive, if perhaps somewhat naïve, scenographic effect which allowed the old quadrangle to retain something of its sense of enclosure and which he was to explore in more archeological Gothic on subsequent occasions.

Wyatt's proposal to open up a long vista at Magdalen is an *al fresco* equivalent to what he notoriously strove to achieve in a number of medieval cathedrals, where his concern to remove internal subdivisions such as screens is sometimes seen as a symptom of the Picturesque. But it was the fact that Holdsworth's scheme was left so incomplete, and remained so into the age of the Picturesque, that enabled the college to start considering a different option to the traditional Oxford approach of completely enclosed courts. This may have been a fashionable response to the writings of Richard Payne Knight and Uvedale Price, [16] or it may have been a very belated acknowledgement of the influence of a former alumnus of the English landscape movement, Joseph Addison, who was a member of the college from 1689-1711.

In 1801 two more figures of national standing entered the lists, submitting related but apparently independent schemes. Humphrey Repton, assisted by his son John Adey Repton, seems to have been first off the mark, since his Red Book is dated January 1st (although it may not have been submitted until October, the date of the postscript), while John Nash's drawings appear to have arrived in July. Both men proposed the basic idea of changing the axis of the second quadrangle from north-south to

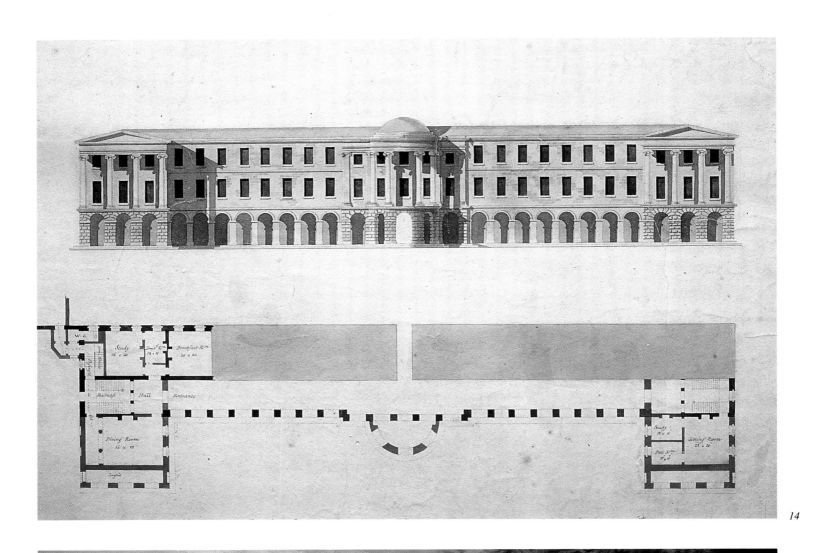

14

15

east-west, incorporating the New Building into a three-sided court open towards the east. In Oxford terms this was not an entirely novel approach since both Trinity and New College had late 17th century quads open on one side towards a garden, and it had also been adopted in the rebuilding of Worcester begun in 1720. At Magdalen, however, as Repton pointed out, previous architects had shown a total disregard for particular advantages it enjoyed (to a greater degree than any other college at either university) in terms of its spacious and well-wooded site, and in designing fully enclosed quadrangles had turned their backs on the river and meadow to the east.

Repton was first and foremost a landscape designer, and his landscaping proposals for Magdalen are more striking than the architectural component, which was in any case largely the responsibility of his son. Noting that the meadow was so damp and often flooded, he proposed that it might as well be treated as a lake, in the process moving the body of water further away from the college. This would be achieved by excavating part of the meadow and diverting the river through it, the spoil being used to raise the encircling walks above flood level and to create a semicircular lawn extending out from the open end of the quadrangle. He then turned his attention to the college appraoches. The general entrance would always be from the High Street, and here he recommended replacing the 'heavy and incongruous' baroque portal with a Gothic gate and open iron palisade; in line with his general desire to open up views, a section of the range fronting the High Street might also be removed to allow a sight of the south flank of the chapel and hall, while the view into St John's Quad would be deepened by the removal of the President's Lodgings. And since the college had hitherto turned its back on the deer park, another potential visual asset might be exploited by creating a new entrance for public and ceremonial occasions at the angle of Longwall and Holywell Streets, leading the visitor in through an embattled lodge and round towards a new gate tower in the centre of the New Building by means of a long, curving drive – very much as he might have dealt with the approach to a country house.

Having re-ordered the environs of the college – as usual, by the simple but always persuasive device of moveable flaps to put across the before-and-after effect – Repton proceeded to address the 'great question' of architectural style:

In the proposed new Buildings, what stile and character should be adopted? Should they accord with the original date of the tower, the chapel, the hall, the cloister &c. called Gothic? Or should they assimilate with the present

New Buildings . . . in the stile called Grecian Architecture? I do not hesitate in saying that the first should be preferred, and of course the Grecian buildings should be Gothick.

The New Building is accordingly, for the first but not the last time, shown refronted in Tudor Gothic and pierced by a fan-vaulted gate tower whose arch would frame a view south (via a single-storey Gothic screen, as previously proposed by Buckler) to the bell tower – from this point seen on axis but set at a slight diagonal. By this *coup d'oeil* the visitor was enabled to savour the 'effect of displaying the parts of a Gothic structure in succession and under various circumstances of perspective and relative distance'.

Magdalen's very own dilemma of style prompted Repton to an extended musing on the comparative qualities of Gothic and classical which was later printed in his *Observations on the Theory and Practice of Landscape Gardening* (1803). One of the characteristics he particularly noted in medieval Gothic buildings was a studied irregularity aimed at producing 'increased grandeur by the intricacy and variety of its parts'. In practice, despite the studied irregularity of his landscape proposals, Reptonian Gothic was notable for its regularity, and, except for the absence of an east side, his Great Quadrangle was arranged with much the same symmetry as Wyatt's. This was largely inevitable, of course, in the case of the refronted New Building, with its two tiers of rectangular sash windows under square Tudor drip-moulds. The latter incongruity was excused on grounds of convenience (Repton claiming, without much conviction, that sashes were no more incongruous on Gothic than classical buildings), though he did also suggest seven different ways of inserting stone mullions and tracery into the frames.

In fact the Reptons were not out-and-out Goths, any more than Wyatt or Nash, and like many architects of their generation their classical designs were often more convincing. The Red Book goes so far as to praise the simplicity and utility of the New Building, and the way in which its form followed its function (a key characteristic of true Gothic buildings, in Repton's view and that of later 19th-century Goths). Indeed, the Postscript of October 1801 alludes to additional designs for completing the quadrangle in the 'Grecian' style, one of them involving a new domed centrepiece for the New Building. Since the designs in question are not included in the Red Book, the reference may relate to a separate unsigned plan and elevation (Fig 14) in which a New Building extended by the addition of a domed centrepiece and porticoed returns faces across lawns to a north cloister range made symmetrical by

16

17

the addition of a Gothic extension at each end. It is a much less ambitious project, but it might well have been more successful and certainly more practical.

JC Buckler, who evidently had free access to the muniment room, was to characterise the offerings of Repton and Nash as 'touched with the artist's magic pencil . . . yet, by their preposterous absurdity, not to enlarge on their ruinous splendour, consigned to . . . oblivion'. Of the two, Nash's scheme, as represented by a set of three dazzling perspectives (Figs 15, 16, 17) attributed to his French draughtsman Auguste Pugin, is undoubtedly the more spectacular in architectural terms, with that tendency to the flashy and theatrical so typical of the Prince Regent's architect. He too saw the opportunity to open the college out to embrace the wider landscape, offering at least three variant plans on the same open-ended theme as Repton had advanced (Figs 18, 19, 20). The perspectives relate to the most ambitious, in which a gap in the centre of the west range frames a new President's Lodgings, detached and villa-like. All is clothed in the same extravagantly modelled Gothic, bristling with pinnacles and ogee-domed turrets that would have lent the Magdalen skyline more than a touch of Xanadu.

Wyatt seems quickly to have got wind of competition – and, moreover, the nature of it – for in February 1801 he wrote to Routh about some very recent thoughts:

> I have made an arrangement or rather disposition of the buildings different from that which I suggested when I was at Oxford, which enables me to avail myself of the beautiful grounds and meadows which surround the College in a way that will add cheerfulness as well as magnificence to the whole.

Although the drawings in question have not previously been identified, it may be that Wyatt's 1801 scheme relates to a pair of unsigned perspectives showing the New Building connected to the old quadrangle not by continuous ranges of accommodation but by single-storey Greek Doric colonnades.[17] That to the west is shown backed by a solid wall articulated by blind arcading, while that on the east opens via a transparent arcade towards the water meadows. A sense of enclosure for the quadrangle is thereby combined with an awareness of the landscape setting – 'cheerfulness as well as magnificence' perhaps. The New Building is given added dignity and focus by a simple applied portico (Ionic above Doric), while in the view south the architect has adopted Buckler's idea of a single-storey Gothic screen between new Gothic ranges at the re-entrant angles. Both the positioning of the latter, and the simplified Gothic, follow Wyatt's 1791 scheme.

Although Wyatt's proposals were, like those of Nash, Repton and a good many other architects, destined to be consigned to the college archives, Dr Routh did not lose interest in the general proposition. In particular he seems to have become fixated with the idea of opening up a view from the New Building into the old quadrangle. John Buckler was recurrently prevailed on to produce ideas as to how this might be done, evidently against his better judgement and certainly against that of his antiquarian-minded son. One of his sketches for a single-storey screen in place of the north cloister range is dated 1804 (Fig 21), the same year in which he submitted a charming idea for a curved Gothic screen to replace the baroque High Street gate and suggested a straightforward method of completing the New Building as an isolated block with short southward-projecting returns.

Further years of inaction passed, until in 1820-21 Buckler was again prompted by the President to return to the subject of the 'view'. Assured by Routh (according to JC Buckler) that 'he should not be answerable as a promoter of the Innovation', he somewhat reluctantly came up with further versions of the single-storey screen (Fig 22), together with more ideas for High Street gateways and for either remodelling the President's Lodging or rebuilding them altogether further to the north (Figs 23, 24).

The President's renewed, if temporary, determination to resolve some of Magdalen's long-standing planning quandaries ushered in the most intensive period of debate and dissension in the college's architectural history, during which the dilemma of style at least reached a decisive climax. Although Wyatt, Repton and Nash had all seemed to favour Gothic for contextual reasons, their willingness (and indeed that of the elder Buckler) to supply classical alternatives was characteristic of the age. Meanwhile, however, there appears to have been a growing groundswell among the fellows that new contributions must not only be Gothic, but correctly so. JC Buckler in 1823 recalled that although the somewhat cavalier, and distinctly unarchaeological, approach of Wyatt had at first seemed irresistible, the combined and steady efforts of eminent antiquaries such as Gough and Carter 'slowly but at last effectually checked the tide of Innovation; and they lived to see their most ardent wishes realised in the overthrow of the most specious, and therefore, most dangerous system that ever invaded the province of taste'. Buckler conceded that 'the ancients' had altered their buildings to suit the prevailing taste, a practice which the enlightened 19th-century might regret but not censure, but he did not allow that this approach to old buildings was any longer permissible. The best modern structures, moreover, would in his view be those which were closest in approach nearest to

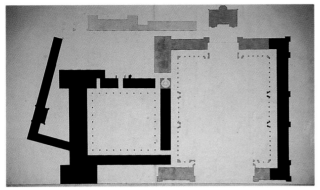

18

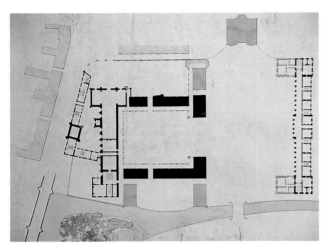

19

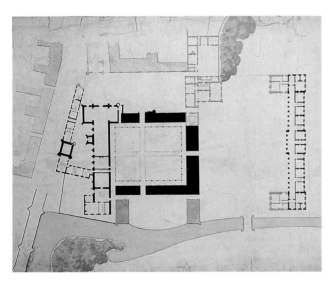

20

21

medieval models.

At the same time that Routh was prompting Buckler's collection of sketch proposals, the college was simultaneously consulting two other architects, both men with a predominantly classical track record. In December 1821 it appointed as consultant Joseph Parkinson, a London-based architect whose most prominent handiwork was the stuccoed classical facades of Montagu and Bryanston Squares. Considerably more distinguished was Thomas Harrison of Chester, an ageing neo-classicist trained in Rome and best known for his important Greek Revival work at Chester Castle. He had however worked quite successfully in a Gothic idiom at Lancaster Castle in the 1790s and at St Nicholas Church in Liverpool in 1811-15. Harrison was consulted early in 1822, and on the basis partly of a visit paid to the college some years previously and partly of the Buckler drawings sent up to Chester by Routh, he felt able to recommend the adoption of Gothic. Plans submitted by him later that year include a refronted New Building and a block to stand at right-angles to it on the west – both in a rather dull pasteboard Gothic, the latter enlivened only by a canted centre and open octagonal cupola. Perhaps he sensed that the designs lacked conviction; at any event his expressed preference for contextual Gothic did not prevent him sending in an alternative design for a handsome new neo-classical block dignified by an Ionic order supported on Tuscan pilasters. This seems to relate to a similar block shown in an interesting undated watercolour, whose most striking feature is a new President's Lodging in the form of a freestanding Greek Doric temple. Such temple forms were not uncommon by the 1820s, but in the Magdalen context the effect is disconcerting to say the least.

Parkinson too demonstrated his classical competence, submitting in 1823 a proposal to make the New Building more imposing by the addition of porticoes (Fig 25). At about the same time the obscure architect Samuel Henry Benham seems to have made a half-hearted effort to get in on the Magdalen act, for his name is on an unfinished but very competent pencil elevation of a New Building remodelled in neo-Greco style by the addition of a trio of elegant pedimented porticoes. Parkinson's main role at this time, however, was to act almost as Routh's stooge in procuring the removal of the north cloister range in the interests of creating the 'view'. His report in mid-1822 (disputed by Buckler junior and also by Henry Hakewill, who was called in subsequently to give an independent opinion) that the range was in a dangerous condition was used as a justification for immediate implementation of the plan for a single-storey screen.[18] Demolition work began at 4am one morning and before anyone had a chance to object all but the cloister itself was down. This precipitate action had the unexpected and indeed unprecedented effect of stirring up public controversy (fuelled, anonymously, by the outraged JC Buckler), to such an extent that a stormy fellows' meeting resulted in an order to cease work. There was a rapid re-think, and by September Routh was assuring a concerned correspondent (somewhat disingenuously) that, 'we have taken down that part of the north side of the old quadrangle which faces the new building, in order to re-edify it exactly in the same style in which it was originally built'.

In fact Routh, hankering after even a partial vista, still hoped that the high pitched roof could be omitted in rebuilding, but in the event the college followed the Bucklers' long-standing idea that the range should be returned to its original form minus the later cocklofts.

The seemingly intractable problem of what to do about the New Building remained, but with the destruction by fire in January 1820 of many of the Magdalen Hall buildings, and the migration of the Hall to the site of Hertford College in 1822, the realisation dawned that it would be possible to side-step the problem. The college was at last able to acquire the coveted land in the angle of the High Street and Longwall Street, and to transfer to it its thoughts of future development (Fig 26). The ragged ends of the New Building were finally faced up straightforwardly in ashlar in 1824 (to a design worked out by Harrison and Parkinson but following closely Buckler's idea of 20 years earlier), and it was accepted that it would for ever remain out on a limb (Fig 27).

From here on, since it was no longer necessary to take the New Building into account, classicism (including even the half-way house of Jacobethan adopted at some other colleges) ceased to be an option, and the question became rather one of which particular variety of Gothic should be adopted. Notwithstanding his claim to have 'taken every possible opportunity to make myself acquainted with the particular style of architecture of Magdalen College', and his avowed belief that 'no alteration or addition should take place but in strict accordance with its present style', Parkinson's Gothic – thin, flat and at times undeniably bleak – was decidedly pre-archaeological in character and altogether lacking in that concern for authenticity which animated the rising generation of Goths such as JC Buckler. He seems, however, to have been an amiable, if uninspired man (Buckler identifies his main qualities as 'great good nature, and ignorance of "Gothic" architecture') and it may be for this reason that, despite the debacle of 1822, his involvement in the

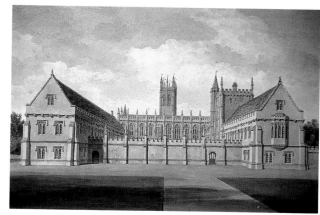

22

23

24

25

26

27

30

college continued into the 1840s. His designs for adding a turreted and castellated block of rooms to the river front of the cloister quadrangle mercifully remained on paper, as did his 1826 scheme for a new President's Lodging and enlarged St John's Quad, but he was entrusted with rebuilding and refitting the old library in 1823-24, giving it its present Gothic oak fittings and a ribbed plaster ceiling that was taken down in 1941 as a precaution against fire-bombs. [19]

In 1822 Francis Goodwin – clearly an architect with his ear to the ground – was the first to put forward ideas for developing the Magdalen Hall site, sending in an ambitious (Buckler calls it 'vast and gaudy') and unsolicited scheme which might have appealed more to the fellows had they not just contributed over £12,000 to rebuilding Hertford College. Apart from envisaging a sizeable new Lodgings at the north-west angle of a much enlarged St John's Quad (the source, infact, with Buckler's 1825 proposal, for Parkinson's scheme), Goodwin's scheme is interesting for proposing to connect the old college buildings to one end of the New Building by a Gothic cloister.[20] This would present a blank wall to the west, concealed by a plantation. The object, explained the architect, 'has been to detach as much as possible these buildings erected in styles of architecture differing in appearance so very much from each other, or rather it has been attempted to prevent the possibility of contrasting the buildings together'.

Although during the 1820s the accession of the Magdalen Hall site seemed set to generate nearly as many optimistic and unfulfilled schemes as had the Great Quadrangle site, shortage of funds meant that in practice the college turned to more modest projects. Parkinson was involved in most of them. In 1824 the curvaceous Jacobean end gable of the High Street range was restored to its triangular medieval form,[21] while in 1825 and 1827 respectively the east and south cloister walks were substantially rebuilt under Parkinson's direction. In 1828 most of the Magdalen Hall Grammar School, which lay along the west side of St John's Quad, was demolished and Parkinson and Buckler seem to have collaborated in tidying up and making more picturesque the belfry turret of 1614 which remained (Fig 28). The decision to retain the turret, which in planning and functional terms was hardly rational, was taken 'on account of its antiquity and unusual shape'. The prime mover, according to the younger Buckler, was Routh – perhaps chastened by the furore over the north cloister range, perhaps merely displaying a characteristic inconsistency. Either way, it was a decision which demonstrated a growing self-consciousness about the picturesqueness of the college ensemble

and which was to have a very practical and arguably not entirely desirable consequence for future development.

In 1828 the college turned its attention to the chapel, and to the question of how to complete the re-Gothicising of the interior begun by Wyatt. Rather than hand the job to Parkinson it was decided (perhaps under prompting from the potentially troublesome JC Buckler) to advertise for applicants, with a reward of 100 guineas for the successful candidate. Of 18 designs submitted, those by Lewis Cottingham were chosen (Fig 29). Cottingham, who had already established his scholarly credentials with books on Westminster Hall, Henry VII's Chapel at Westminster Abbey and on medieval Gothic ornament, was an architect of genuine antiquarian interests and consequently, in the aftermath of 1822, very much the sort of man Magdalen thought it needed. His approach to the chapel was perhaps more thorough-going than the fellows might originally have envisaged, since it involved undoing all that had been done only 40 years previously. Wyatt's pretty, if incorrect, plaster vault was replaced by a simple ribbed affair, and all the miscellaneous fittings – stalls, panelling, reredos, organ screen – were turned out to make way for others of unimpeachable if mechanical correctitude. The east wall was given a reredos of tiered niches (originally empty but filled in 1865 with figures carved by Thomas Earp to designs by Clayton and Bell) culminating in a relief of Christ meeting Mary Magdalen, executed under the direction of Sir Francis Chantrey. Though the total effect was undoubtedly more homogeneous than hitherto (in 1830 Cottingham emphasised to the fellows his view that to retain any of the old fittings would detract from the desired 'uniformity of effect'), one cannot with hindsight help regretting the loss of the carved classical woodwork listed for sale in a 1837 auctioneer's catalogue.[22] The transformation was completed in 1856-57, when the controversial Eginton glass in the antechapel was banished, along with the two Price windows, and replaced by the 1630s monochrome figures from the choir. The space thus vacated was filled with brightly coloured glass by Hardman. It may have been at this time that Sir George Gilbert Scott supplied a sketch idea for alleviating the distinctly bleached effect of the Cottingham interior by giving the vault an overlay of poly-chrome decoration.[23]

The re-Gothicising of Magdalen was completed in 1844 with the long-mooted replacement of the classical entrance gate, for which so many different proposals had been advanced from Wyatt onwards. In 1828 Buckler senior had written to Routh that 'the old gateway looks more obnoxious than ever; it

will be impossible to endure it any length of time'. Rather surprisingly the commission eventually went not to Buckler or his son but – at the intercession of a prominent Anglo-Catholic fellow, Dr John Bloxam – to AWN Pugin, then smarting from the rejection of his designs for Balliol the previous year. Pugin professed a deep and undoubtedly genuine admiration for Magdalen, though he could not conceive 'how the society with such a glorious model before them could have erected the Italian Barrack in the park', and it was appropriate that his only Oxford work, albeit a minor one, should be for the college. It was, sadly, to survive less than 40 years, being demolished rather unnecessarily in 1883 to make way for the new St Swithun's Quad.

Given all the architectural huffing and puffing that had gone on since Wyatt's 1791 proposal, it says much about the Magdalen time-scale that the college's first substantial new building did not go up until 1849. Moreover, the whole of this long period of intermittent and unproductive ferment had been compassed by the reign of Dr Routh, who on his 94th birthday laid the foundation stone of a new Choristers' Hall on the site of the old Greyhound Inn at the corner of High Street and Longwall (Fig 30). Here at last was JC Buckler's opportunity to show what he could do, and he acquitted himself with a very creditable essay in Perpendicular Gothic that must have gladdened both his dying father and the fabulously antique President.[24] Buckler's other notable contribution to the college was in fact the design of Routh's monumental brass, placed before the chapel altar following his death in 1854.

Buckler himself outlived even Routh, dying in 1894 at the age of 100. When in 1879 the fellows finally got round to organising a limited competition for the development of the Magdalen Hall site, he was not invited to participate (perhaps on account of his already very advanced years), but his admonitions of more than half a century before seem to have resounded in the ears of both competitors and assessors. Buckler had in 1823 cast doubt on the efficiency of architectural competitions, commenting drily on the difficulty of getting 40 fellows to agree on the best scheme in consequence of the fact that 'the study of architecture forms no part of education, and taste therein slumbers almost undisturbed within the walls of both Universities'. Nevertheless, by 1879 the basic approach which he advocated had long since become common ground: 'Magnificence must be forgotten; it is already possessed by Magdalen College in the highest degree; she requires subordinate additions, not rival fabrics'. In this spirit all four competitors – Basil Champneys, George Edmund Street, William Wilkinson and the firm of Bodley and Garner –

though each normally capable of very considerable originality, consciously forewent the temptation to do other than (in Champneys' words) 'follow as closely as possible the spirit of the ancient buildings'.

The Magdalen competition did not bring out the best in Champneys, who was simultaneously designing Newnham College at Cambridge in a very attractive Dutch-influenced red brick. He was later to practice an equally attractive 'free Gothic' with Arts and Crafts touches, at New College (1896) and Merton (1904-10), but in 1879 was too early for the Arts and Crafts and at Magdalen he produced a curiously dull, over-cautious design that was also too large for the available site.[25] Street's entry fell between two stools, renouncing his preferred 13th-century idiom without altogether mastering Magdalen's Perpendicular. Perhaps the most completely successful scheme in planning terms was that of Wilkinson (Fig 31), who had already left his mark on Oxford with the Randolph Hotel of 1864 and whose stylistic allegiance was, like Street, to an earlier Gothic. He proposed a much enlarged St John's Quad, with new Lodgings on the north side and an L-shaped range bounding the west and south. Pugin's gate was retained, but a new principal entrance was provided by an imposing gate tower enlivened by a two-tier oriel window (the latter a feature found on all four submissions). It was in fact a disposition not unlike that advanced by Goodwin, but both schemes were handicapped by the fact that they involved the removal of the Grammar Hall to which so much misplaced sentiment was now attached. Bodley and Garner, on the other hand, clearly struck a sympathetic chord in their emphatic statement that 'no plan ought to be adopted that would remove this picturesque old work'.

Bodley and Garner's winning entry (Figs 32, 33) is not a bad design in elevational terms, though it makes no claim to particular originality, 'Our elevations do not . . . copy or reproduce the old work. That would be a mistake, and would confuse the history of the buildings. But we have aimed at designing in the old manner and in harmony with the spirit of the old work'. The problem, from a planning point of view, is that the retention of the Grammar Hall meant keeping a St John's Quad whose western boundary was still that of the old dividing line between College and Hall, with an entirely new quad created outside it. That quad was to have been surrounded and enclosed in the traditional manner, with contiguous ranges around the north, south and west sides, and the Grammar Hall sitting somewhat pointlessly on the east sandwiched between a crenellated wall and an open iron screen. As implemented in 1880-84 only the south side and part of

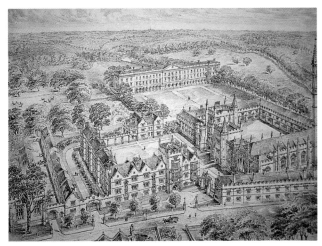

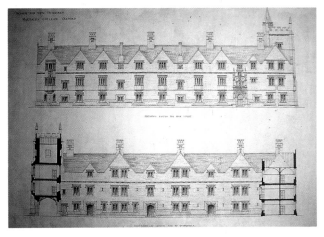

the west side were built, and when in 1928 Sir Giles Gilbert Scott was brought in to resume work he chose not to add the missing north range but to create a dog-leg by heading westwards for the Longwall boundary across land recently vacated by Magdalen College School. It was then, and not before, that Magdalen created its 'tradition' of deliberately, rather than accidentally, incomplete and open-ended spaces.

Having failed to enlarge St John's Quad westwards, in 1888 the college passed up the chance of enlarging it northwards by having Bodley and Garner rebuild and enlarge the President's Lodgings on its old site. The idiom adopted was, needless to say, in the deferential mould outlined by Buckler in the 1820s. [26] Scott's vocabulary of 1928 was an uncontroversial and largely uneventful simplification of domestic Tudor, and unfortunately his sole attempt at originality – a gateway to Longwall in what Colvin aptly calls 'deliquescent Gothic' (the Gothic, that is, of his Liverpool Cathedral designs) – was left unexecuted. So too was his design of 1936 for a new gateway in Flamboyant Gothic to supercede Bodley and Garner's rather dull affair to the High.

In retrospect it is hard not to conclude that, of Magdalen's 500 or so years of architectural evolution, at least 250 have been dogged by that fateful decision in 1731 to proceed with an over-ambitious scheme in a style completely at odds with that of the original nucleus. Lack of funds, lack of real need and lack of determination meant that full implementation failed to take place during the decades when it was psychologically possible – that is, before the growth of antiquarian sentiment and the advance of the Gothic Revival made it impossible to tamper with the Founder's work without generating more public controversy than the college wished to contemplate. A good deal has been made of the baneful role played in this long saga of indecision and misjudgement by Dr Routh, who clung tenaciously to a concept first adumbrated by Wyatt and yet was said (by Buckler) to 'recoil before even a feeble opposition'. In fact, from an architectural and planning point of view Routh inherited an exceptionally perplexing problem that taxed a succession of eminent imaginations, and it may in fairness be felt that the odds were already stacking up against its resolution by him or anybody else. It must also be remembered that any president, however strongminded, would have faced an uphill task in carrying with him a body of independent-minded and often contrary fellows.

Leaving aside the element of indecision endemic in Oxbridge building projects, one could argue that, at least since the 1820s, Magdalen has been able to proceed in an increasingly, self-consciously picturesque and space-consumptive fashion only because it enjoys grounds of exceptional spaciousness. The more general moral, perhaps, is that for reasons which may be regrettable but are also both explicable and predictable, grand designs are almost always bound to fail in a collegiate context; money is rarely available for their full and immediate implementation, and taste is apt to move on faster than the funding. Whether the implication of this fact of Oxbridge life is that architects should strive for homogeneity by clinging to an architectural tradition, or whether it is enough to be satisfied with more diverse juxtapositions, is a question far from resolved in the 1990s. It is interesting to note that although Magdalen's most recent addition of any size, the Waynflete Building of 1960-61, was in a stolid and deeply unmemorable version of an idiom then considered 'modern', the college would undoubtedly have acquired a building of much greater individuality had it gone ahead in 1947 with Oliver Hill's scheme to redevelop land on the Botanic Garden side of the High Street in an ostensibly conservative neo-Georgian. Hill's originality lies not so much in his elevations as in his striking plan, in which Nicholas Stone's Botanic Garden gate of 1632-33 becomes the highly-modelled focus of a gently-curving two-part crescent, with accommodation raised up above transparent ground-floor colonnades. It is a plan which seems, consciously or otherwise, to pick up the threads where Hawksmoor, with his concern for curves, colonnades and axiality, left off. From the centre of the crescent Hill's site plan shows an axis passing, like an invisible ley-line, across the High Street and through the medieval nucleus to strike the centre of the New Building – almost as if he is suggesting that the agonisings and uncertainties of the intervening 200 years had been an unnecessary distraction.

Notes

I wish to thank Dr Janie Cottis (Magdalen College Archivist) and Howard Colvin for their help and advice in the preparation of this short survey.

1 Howard Colvin, *Unbuilt Oxford*, 1983. The other principal sources for an architectural history of Magdalen College, apart from the material in the college archives, are: TSR Boase, 'An Oxford College and the Gothic Revival' (*Journal of the Warburg and Courtauld Institutes*, Vol XVIII, Nos 3 & 4, 1955; Royal Commission on Historical Monuments, *City of Oxford*, 1939; JC Buckler, *Observations on the Original Architecture of St Mary Magdalen College, Oxford*; and on the *Innovations Anciently or Recently Attempted*, 1823.

2 Indeed the RCHM Oxford inventory of 1939 suggests that there is evidence to indicate that the Magdalen quadrangle may originally have been planned without cloister walks.

3 The gate was inevitably attributed subsequently to Inigo Jones and more recently to Nicholas Stone; it now proves to be the work of the Christmas family of mason-carvers (payment in college archives).

4 Those at Magdalen were added to the north cloister range and, as several Buckler drawings show, were a prominent object in the view from the New Building. They disappeared as a consequence of the controversial rebuilding of the range in 1822-24.

5 Howard Colvin, *Catalogue of Architectural Drawings of the 18th and 19th Centuries in the Library of Worcester College, Oxford*, 1964.

6 In April 1734 he wrote to Dr Butler from Bath with practical suggestions, adding that 'as I am very frequently thinking of your building it may happen that some little conveniencies may from time to time occur to me, wch you will give me leave to communicate to you, tho' never so trivial . . . I hope my Brother has acquainted you wth what I desir'd him concerning a proper place for powdering wigs in every staircase'.

7 Howard Colvin points out that an incoming fellow paid his predecessor a proportion of the cost the latter had incurred, usually in wainscotting old rooms.

8 JC Buckler, *Observations*.

9 *Ibid*.

10 RD Middleton, *Dr Routh*, 1938. At the end of his life there were said to be parts of the college which Routh had never visited.

11 As, for instance, the anomalous status of Gentleman Commoners or the practice of Demies retaining their scholarships indefinitely until a fellowship became vacant.

12 Being paid for by a legacy from Dr West; it later came to be known as 'the Gothics'.

13 Townesend was the last practising member of that Oxford architectural dynasty. The bog-house was subdivided hierarchically into compartments for fellows, Demies and servants (the last category being provided with a continuous five-seater).

14 He estimated the total number of his sketches at more than 13,000.

15 The three-sided front quadrangle at Queen's (1709-34) is screened from the street by a single-storey cloister range, an arrangement found in some Tudor and Jacobean mansions and also in Parisian townhouses.

16 Richard Payne Knight, *The Landscape, A Didactic Poem*, 1794; Uvedale Price, *An Essay on the Picturesque*, 1794.

17 Wyatt, according to Professor J Mordaunt Crook, is otherwise known to have used pure Greek Doric only twice, at Gresford Lodge, Denbigh *c*1790 and at Ottershaw Park, Surrey *c*1800. On the Canterbury Quad gate at Christ Church of 1773-83 he used a somewhat hybrid Roman-Greek Doric variety.

18 Harrison too had written in July 1822 in support of the idea.

19 The present panelled ceiling dates from 1954 (*ex inf* Howard Colvin).

20 Goodwin's Lodgings would have provided as much accommodation as a medium-sized country house, including a large service wing with servants' hall.

21 Buckler in 1823 referred to the classical doorcase to the cloister passage as having been recently removed.

22 Two small panels of carving in the Grinling Gibbons manner survive in the President's Lodgings.

23 The sketch is unsigned and undated, but an attached label bears the word 'Scott'. Sir George Gilbert Scott died in 1878. Also in the archives is a plan (ref H25, inscribed GG Scott RA, Architect/ 51 Spring Gardens, London) for developing the Magdalen Hall site.

24 The school was moved to the other side of Magdalen Bridge in 1894 but the hall remained in use as a school room until 1933 when it was converted into a library and absorbed into the new Longwall Quad.

25 Champneys' other major work in Oxford was Mansfield College (1887-89).

26 Bodley's last contribution to the college was the removal in 1903 of Wyatt's plaster vault to the Hall, replacing it with an archaeological reconstruction of the original timber roof.

DAVID WATKIN

PUTTING A HUMAN HEAD ON A HORSE'S NECK [1]

When introducing new buildings into historic settings we need to consider what will be appropriate in character rather than concentrating on issues of style. It thus turns out that building in such areas is little different from building anywhere else. In this context we will find helpful the classical discussion of character in poetry and rhetoric which connects men as far removed as Aristotle and Soane. [2] For the Greek philosopher Aristotle, there were three types of poetry, epic, dramatic and lyrical. It is important to realise that, though each was described as a style, the term did not have the connotations of a personal artistic language which it has acquired in the modern world. Quite the reverse, it represented a common language, or genre, whose appropriateness was universally perceived as fitting to the task in hand.

The Roman poet Horace was indebted to Aristotle for the principle of decorum which was fundamental to his *Ars Poetica*. Horace's doctrine of literary propriety or fitness was based on the theory of rhetoric in which different types of oratory were thought appropriate to different occasions. Cicero in the *Brutus* and *The Orator* defined two distinct styles of good oratory, one simple and the other elevated, and in his *De Oratore* he introduced a middle style between grand and plain. Horace made such an approach the guiding principle of his *Ars Poetica*. He begins by postulating:

> Supposing a painter chose to put a human head on a horse's neck, or to spread feathers of various colours over the limbs of several different creatures, or to make what is in the upper part a beautiful woman tail off into a hideous fish, could you help laughing when he showed you his efforts?

Later, he argues that, 'the banquet of Thyestes cannot be fitly described in the strains of everyday life or in those that approach the tone of comedy, Let each of these styles be kept for the role properly allotted to it.' [3]

Horace's vivid image of a human head on a horse's neck immediately suggests to our minds the architectural analogy of the foolish juxtaposition of a modern building of incongruous form in a setting of totally contrasting character. One striking example is David Roberts' Sacher Building (1961-62) at New College, Oxford, described by Professor Crook

as the product of an architect 'blinded by non-visual dogma.' [4] Certainly, the manifest inappropriateness of this brutal building in the historic curved street to which its uncompromising severity is a deliberately graceless affront, makes one cry rather than, with Horace, laugh.

The humanist art theorists of the Renaissance had already inverted Horace's tag, '*Ut Pictura poesis*' (as with painting, so with poetry), and applied it so that painting could be governed by the rules of classical poetics. In the 18th century, the French architect Germain Boffrand [5] and Robert Morris, [6] the leading architectural philosopher of his generation in Britain, had the idea of transferring the rules of rhetoric from painting to architecture. [7] Boffrand did this in the section entitled 'Principes tirés de l'art poétique d'Horace' in his *Livre d'architecture contenant les principes généraux de cet art* (1745), and Morris in his *The Art of Architecture: a poem in imitation of Horace's The Art of Poetry* (1742).

The attack in late 17th-century France by Claude Perrault on the origin in divine harmony of the proportions of the orders had left a gap which 18th-century theorists sought to fill. Now that architecture had ceased to be a divine language, it became, in their hands, a human one. The pioneers in this shift were Boffrand, his follower JF Blondel and Morris. Boffrand went so far as to paraphrase Horace's text, relating it to architecture in 29 parallel passages:

> Architecture . . . though its object seems only to be the use of what is material, is capable of different types which serve to animate its basic solutions by means of the different characters that it can express . . . A building, by its composition, expresses itself as on a stage that the scene is pastoral or tragic, that it is a temple or a palace, a public building destined for a specific use or a private house. These different buildings, through their disposition structure and the manner in which they are decorated, should announce their purpose to the spectator; and if they do not do so, they sin against expression and are not what they should be. [8]

Fundamental to all of Robert Morris' numerous written works, including his *Lectures on Architecture* (1734 and 1736), and his *Essay on Harmony*

OPPOSITE: Rob Krier, Amiens, The square between the former Bishop's palace (right) and the Faculty of Law: framing the axis is the portal of the Ponte Vecchio

(1739), is the establishment of harmony between a building and its situation. Blondel, the most influential teacher of architecture in 18th-century Europe, read a paper at the Académie Royale d'Architecture in 1766, entitled 'Essaye sur le caractère qui convient à chaque genre d'édifice', subsequently published in his *Cours d'architecture*.[9] Blondel, who was heavily dependent on Boffrand, developed an anthropomorphic interpretation by which he could speak of male, female, and even dwarf-like character in architecture. His heavy emphasis on character and his accompanying belief in what he called 'the poetry of architecture' was taken up in the sensualist theories proposed by Le Camus de Mézières in his *Le Génie de l'architecture ou l'analogie de cet art avec nos sensations* (1780), and had a dangerous aftermath in the heady fantasies of Ledoux. In his ideal town of Chaux, which did not contain customary urban buildings such as theatre, hospital, market house or museum, Ledoux dethroned architecture in favour of a collectivist fantasy where buildings had become poetic exhortations which did you good by their mere existence.

The new emphasis on architecture as language, as Sylvia Lavin has recently shown,[10] was a process originally rooted in the search in 18th-century discourse for the origins of both architecture and language. This went hand in hand with the quest for first principles, a basic concern of the Enlightenment, which flourished in the writings of Quatremère de Quincy. Sir John Soane studied Quatremère's work in detail, acquiring three copies of his *De l'architecture égyptienne* (1803), and two of his *Encyclopédie méthodique*. In his painful creation of an architectural language of relevance, Soane would have read with interest such pleas by Quatremère as:

> It is extremely important, and I shall not cease from repeating it, that if the language of architecture is to have worth, if its signs are to be understood and are to create the effect of which they are capable . . . it is necessary, in order for them to say something, that one does not employ them to say nothing.[11]

We are only now beginning to understand the passionate search for appropriate character which dominated the professional career of Sir John Soane whose classicism and modernity can offer us valuable hints today about an appropriate architecture. He noted in *c*1812, for example, that:

> The Ancients were as attentive in the application of the different orders as to the situation and distinctive character of their buildings. Vitruvius further tells us that the proportions and symmetry of Columns of Porticos of buildings in general are not to be the same as those prescribed for sacred edifices. These distinc-

tions in the situation and character of buildings constitute, if I may be allowed the expression, the costume of architecture. Attention therefore to costume is as necessary to the architect as to the Painter or the Poet, for although buildings formed by the unions of discordant parts, like Pictures with forced imagery, may have the charms of variety and the powers of novelty, yet such Compositions, although sanctioned by fashion and other meretricious aids, will only obtain ephemeral praise and please the unskilful.[12]

Soane made copious notes from and translations of works by authors who studied the philosophy of character such as Boffrand, Blondel, Morris and Lord Kames. He would not have understood the new and unclassical use of the word style which arose in the 19th century when the 18th-century interest in character became an obsession with the historical associations of different styles.[13]

The 19th-century intellectual tradition which was ultimately hostile to a proper understanding of character and style was the Hegelian concept of the *Zeitgeist*. This encouraged the belief that a building should be 'true to its age' rather than to its situation or function. One of the myths associated with this tradition was the belief that:

> human nature has changed so radically that a new man has been born who must either learn to express himself in a radically new way which is externally dictated by economic and political conditions, or must himself be changed radically in order to conform to these new conditions.[14]

In order to recover appropriate architecture in the post-modern world it is necessary to overturn such beliefs and show that human nature does not alter from generation to generation. Porphyrios' proposed Longwall Quadrangle for Magdalen College, Oxford, ironically opposite Roberts' Sacher Building, marks an important stage in the process of rehabilitation of traditional ideals of decorum. The scheme follows classical rhetorical theory with the public building, a lecture theatre, in the elevated style, which is classical, and the domestic accommodation in the simpler style, vernacular, occupying a lower position in the hierarchy of building genres.

The new British Library is unacceptable because it has nothing to say about its role as guardian of the high dignity of learning and resembles a giant out-of-town supermarket overshadowed in importance by the adjacent station hotel. If by appropriate character we meant contextualism, we would not be able to defend Basevi for having built the Fitzwilliam Museum in Trumpington Street, Cambridge, in the 1830s. Its splendid Corinthian portico towers above the plastered Tudor cottages of the narrow street as an appropriate temple of the arts. Attention to the traditional rhetorical language which has underlain much of our historical architecture will help us to explain why the Fitzwilliam Museum is acceptable and the new British Library is not.

To conclude, we need to cease discussing new developments in historic settings, or indeed in any settings, in terms of historical styles. Instead, we should return to the notion borrowed from classical rhetorical theory that there should be a hierarchy of styles from low to high for different genres of buildings.

Let us return to the Sacher Building: although the contextualist argument is a useful stick with which to beat unrepentant Modernists such as the late David Roberts, it is not in the end the only, or the most important, reason why we condemn the Sacher Building. It offends because its aggressiveness is inappropriate to its modest function.

Notes

1 In preparing this paper I have been indebted to discussion with Mr Richard John of Merton College, Oxford.

2 See GL Hendrikson, 'The Origin and Meaning of the Ancient Characters of Style', *American Journal of Philology,* vol xxvi, 1905.

3 Horace, *Ars Poetica,* trans TS Dorsch, 1965, p79 and 82.

4 JM Crook, *The Dilemma of Style,* 1987, p265.

5 See C Mackenzie, 'The *Ut Poesis Architectura* of Germain Boffrand', PhD thesis, University of Toronto, 1984, and W Rensselaer Lee, *Ut Pictura Poesis: the Humanist Theory of Painting,* New York, 1967.

6 See D Leatherbarrow, 'Architecture and Situation: A Study of the Architectural Writings of Robert Morris', *Journal of the Society of Architectural Historians,* March 1985, xliv, pp48-59; WA Gibson, 'Literary Influences on R Morris' First Excursion in Architectural Theory', *Rendezvous,* Idaho State University Journal of Art and Letters, vii, 1971, no 3, pp1-14.'

7 R Saisselin, *Ut Pictura Poesis,* Journal of Aesthetics and Arts, vol xx, Winter 1966, pp45-57.

8 G Boffrand, *Livre d'Architecture,* 1745, p16.

9 JF Blondel, *Cours d'architecture, 6 vols,* 1771-77, vol ii, pp 229ff.

10 S Lavin, *Quatremère de Quincy and the Invention of a Modern Language of Architecture,* MIT Press, 1992.

11 AC Quatremère de Quincy, *Dictionnaire d'architecture,* 3 vols, in *Encyclopédie méthodique,* ed CJ Panckoucke, 3 vols, Paris 1788-1825, vol l, p508.

12 Sir John Soane's Museum, Soane MSS, MBiii \ 3, ff 4-5.

13 Porphyrios has argued that, 'The question of style . . . does not *exist* in classicism since the individual personality is always informed by the *techne*' (*Classical Architecture,* 1992, p56).

14 DJ Watkin, *Morality and Architecture,* Oxford, 1977, p7.

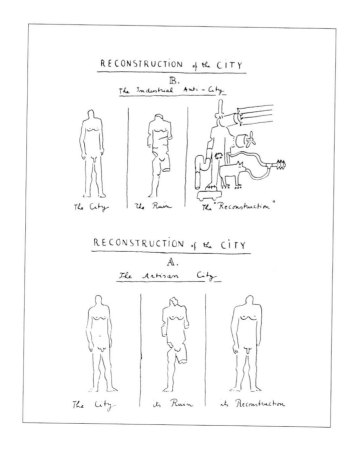

LEFT: Leon Krier, Critique of the Industrial ANTI-CITY

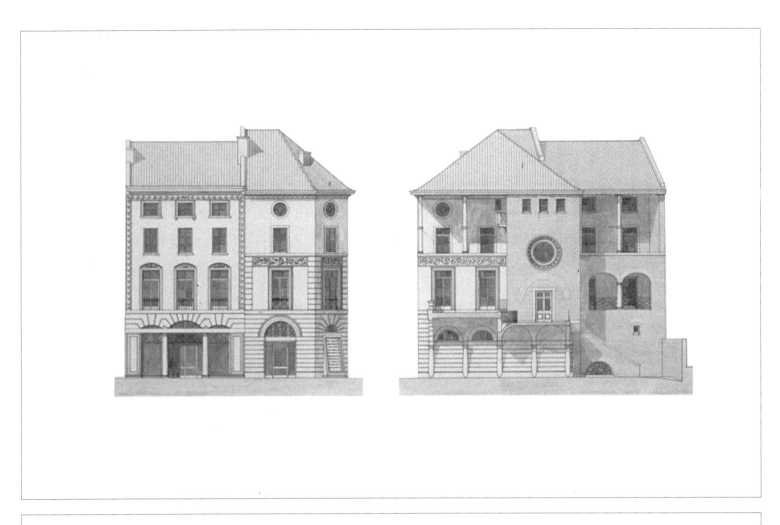

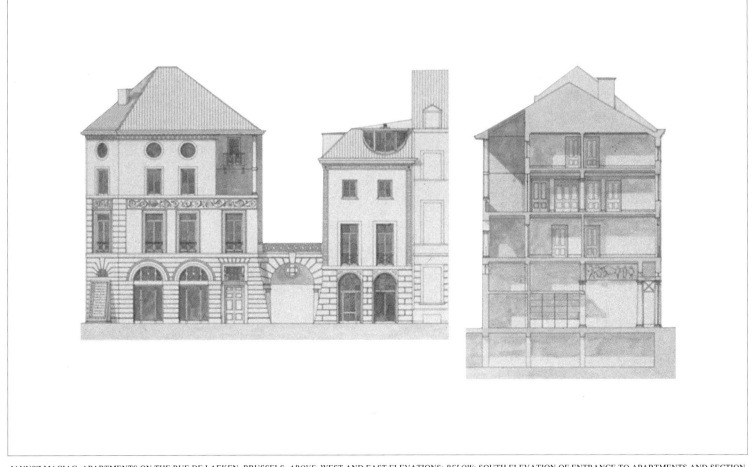

JANUSZ MACIAG, APARTMENTS ON THE RUE DE LAEKEN, BRUSSELS; *ABOVE*: WEST AND EAST ELEVATIONS; *BELOW*: SOUTH ELEVATION OF ENTRANCE TO APARTMENTS AND SECTION

MAURICE CULOT

LUCIDITY VERSUS HUMILITY
(humility is not an architectural virtue)

'The objection to pastiche, absence of originality, the constraint of tradition, attachment to the past and old age is, as a rule, aimed at all that is truly strong and truly great in times of artistic decadence and critical lethargy.'
Gustav Moreau, *The Collector of Dreams*

As the year 2000 draws nearer, castles, palaces, stately homes and imperial residences all over Europe have been catching fire for reasons that seem too insignificant to be true. The supposed negligence of a restorer of paintings, for example, or perhaps a defective switch . . . Windsor, Hofburg, Laeken, Potsdam, Chambord and so many other historic buildings have disappeared like this in flames, the heavy beams from their ballrooms collapsing in cinders onto age-old floors where Europe was first born.

It will be the task of historians of the 21st century to classify all these events and draw their conclusions, to fully assess this cruel century in which the weaknesses of men prevented greatness from emerging; where too many miseries were laid bare, too many breaches of trust were exposed, where there were not enough hypocrisies.

With time, we shall establish that there were already signs there to warn us – but of what? As yet, we can only criticise without being sure, and conclude nothing definite except that we only know too much. But we will undoubtedly also have to take these signs for just what they are, because when the world goes up in flames like this without any apparent reason, and the coincidences multiply, it is always to remind men of the coherence of their world. Nostalgia grabs the more sensitive ones by the throat: how should they react when faced with the heritage of the past? It is at this very moment that one has to draw on the reserves of originality and have ready to hand a little theory. To each his own, then, and in these troubled times I shall take care not to point to the best theory but, rather, merely tell you of my own experience.

Some years ago, I patiently put together a miniature pantheon. It is accurately heterogeneous and acts as both my artistic conscience and spiritual family. Whenever questioned, my dearly departed invariably reply the same thing: 'Be original, dear Maurice: imitate within the narrower limits of your architectural knowledge – that which has been best produced by preceding generations.' Ever since then, since my own art amounts to analysis and words, I advise those who wish to listen to me to have recourse to imitation. I encourage the beginners (which one can still be at the age of 53) to investigate the field of *copy*; the more knowledgeable point towards *pastiche*; to those of Cartesian minds I urge the identical *restoration* of the original; while to those of a whimsical nature, the meanders of *mimesis*. And I would suggest to all of them that they should be responsive to what is delightful, picturesque and pleasant to the eye, to learn the art of patina and *faux-vieux*, and to juggle with moulding techniques and the reproduction of facades, even of whole streets. So with such great vistas to originality open before us, only those truly thoughtless to any notion of imagination can still attempt to compare them with Disneyland.

If I were asked about my own tastes I would say that I tend towards picturesque and congenial disorder rather than the rigorous order of the drawing-board and the stately coldness of classical palaces. But I do like a mixture of the two – to give you an example in an image: a neo-classical or baroque square surrounded by a system of winding and irregularly laid out streets.

For as one grows older, one becomes, if not an adult, in any case more thoughtful, that is, more receptive to the variety of sensations and emotions that can affect one. One's body becomes more attentive to the pleasures that it gives and receives, to the comfort as well and the warmth which warms one's bones and encourages idleness. Also, being part of the bourgeoisie, one at last appreciates its immeasurable qualities. One looks back with amused interest, and sometimes a little embarrassment, at the years where we always seemed to find inspiration in protest (let alone revolutionary romanticism).

Finally, once one has calmed down, but is none the wiser for it, no longer having any desire to change the world and relieved of any inclination to convince those around one, there does remain one essential thing: the taste for originality. A sensual originality, free from any attachment to and prejudice against anything alluring; like a statue in stone

ABOVE AND BELOW: JOSEPH ALTUNA, VIEWS OF PROJECT FOR THE RECONSTRUCTION OF A BUILDING ON THE RUE DE LA GOUTTE D'OR, PARIS

of a woman with rounded breasts to the Ancients' liking, and not too tall for my own liking, with a sensual, long face, looking down with large eyes – one pensive, the other nearly closed – like the statues at the Trocadero. So, one can breathe a sigh of relief and note that the one's tremendous desire for originality has remained intact, beyond one's rapidly receding hairline and the beginnings of a paunch.

Also, forgive me for not being able to acknowledge the defence of humility for winning architectural battles. For which army wants to fight under such a banner? What sort of victory can it hope for?

The only thing that really matters is that one keeps their freedom of speech and action. I would also say each to their own regarding everything else, and there is an endless list of forms from the past to choose from. As I mentioned earlier, my own tastes tend more towards the picturesque which is better able to absorb any awkwardness and errors of composition that can be so obvious in classicism. And as architects can no longer take advantage of a classical culture, it would be better to limit risks and leave columns, capitals, astragals and pediments in the accessory store.

Firstly, to consider the town as the setting of people's lives seems to me to be consistent with our own humanity rather than anything proposed by partisans of mechanised functionalism. For man needs a civilised architectural framework in order to satisfy his animal nature. Let him have his hope of remission at least. The preservation and maintenance of historic places is, of course, legitimate, but there must also be construction of new areas, new streets and squares, taking the old ones as their models. Whether these are made of plaster or stucco, and whether they hide banal, plain interiors is of no importance. The less we interfere in the sphere of private life, the better it will be for it.

Secondly, let us admit that we do have certain priorities, and the creation of public spaces is one of them. Not public spaces that drive us to despair with their abstraction, but which encourage the young because they display, in their fondness for history, the successes and difficulties of that which has preceded them. They also demonstrate that innovation is no longer to be found in the search for original shapes but, rather, in gaining new freedom and thus in taming ghosts form the past.

By giving priority to the theatre of public life, to the scene in which civil society is produced, one also recognises the importance of the actors, the depth of ideas, the quality of the game, and one makes way for a lively ecology, knowingly mixes real life with fiction, and feigns and resumes a hypocrisy without which life in society is impossible.

Some people have seen in lucidity a blind passion which sees everything and kills everything it sees. It is true that the abuse of lucidity, as with alcoholic abuse, is contrary to the joy of life which remains an essential thing, even in those who might scorn life. Lucidity nowadays seems to me, nevertheless, to constitute one of the final barriers against the trend which is dragging us to a known outcome. It is a key which can unlock the universe or memory – memory of all that has been best produced by previous generations, and which always offers itself to copying and imitation. Let us leave humility, then, to the monasteries and to those whose vocation is Faith.

Whether it be in books, classes or lectures, I plead for the imitation of the beauties and successes of yester-year, and I have the weakness to believe that, one day, the old stones, stuccoes and patinated renderings will whisper as I go past: 'It is he, it is he . . .' or, rather, lowering in pitch our pride: 'It is one of them, it is one of them . . .'

LAURENT CAZALIS, MAURICE CULOT, JEAN PIERRE MAJOT, ELEVATION OF NEW MARKET BUILDING, BAYONNE, FRANCE, 1990

DEMETRI PORPHYRIOS ASSOCIATES
NEW LONGWALL QUADRANGLE, MAGDALEN COLLEGE, OXFORD

The proposal for a new quadrangle for Magdalen College in Oxford comprises residential accommodation for students and a lecture theatre. This is the winning entry in an invited architectural competition.

Unlike any other Oxford College, the buildings of Magdalen College have a singular quality that derives from a constant dialogue between built form and open space. Collegiate planning is generally composed of a series of courts which are bounded by buildings. The open space of a court, therefore, is always experienced as a figure. Magdalen College, however, has a unique quadrangle organisation that is enclosed yet open. St John's, Chaplain's, St Swithun's, Longwall and the New Buildings' Quads are all enclosed spaces, yet their boundaries are soft with open vistas. The siting of the buildings is such that, together with the River Cherwell and the placement of walls, fences, mounds or ha-ha's, a sense of both enclosure and perspectival freedom is achieved.

Any sensible proposal for the New Longwall Quadrangle cannot disregard this 'open grain' in the building fabric of Magdalen College. We took the view, therefore, that we must encourage this interplay between solids and voids and, taking into account the requirements of the brief, we proposed a new quadrangle which re-affirms the urban quality of the adjacent quads while opening up to the east towards the deer-park.

The lecture theatre is placed close to the Longwall Gate thus enhancing the area as a recognisable place of arrival. It is entered through an octagonal open-air pavilion that leads to a sky-lit foyer which functions also as an exhibition space. The theatre proper, a great hall with a raked floor and a trussed oak roof, is a flexible space which features both seating in the round and seating for cinematic projection. The lecture theatre presents itself as an enigmatic camera obscura. Its scale derives from the great round windows that flank its sides between which corbelled volutes are positioned to receive future sculptures.

In siting the residential buildings we broke them down into small units oriented towards the deer park. The hall of residence next to the masonry screen is rotated so that maximum views of the Great Tower are afforded from the Quad and beyond. The Longwall Range has an arcade appended to its east side while the building next to it steps forward slightly to make space for a small service courtyard behind. Residential accommodation is organised in traditional Oxford sets of two or four rooms per landing.

The long and distinguished history of the College engraved in its buildings and skyline has shown us the architectural language with which to compose. The buildings are constructed in masonry walls with ashlar stone externally and plaster with lime paint internally. All exposed timber work is in oak. Roofs are generally in stone slates except that of the theatre which is finished in copper.

The contrast between the classical of the theatre and the vernacular of the halls of residence heightens the dialogue between their public and private nature respectively; thus underlining once more the urban quality of the scheme as a whole and its relation to the existing College. This is not an introverted mega-structural scheme but rather a quadrangle where a number of buildings of different character, dimensions and scale co-exist like members of a family; creating open spaces to be enjoyed by the College community and in harmony with the existing landscape.

PERSPECTIVE VIEW OF AUDITORIUM AND ENTRANCE TO QUADRANGLE

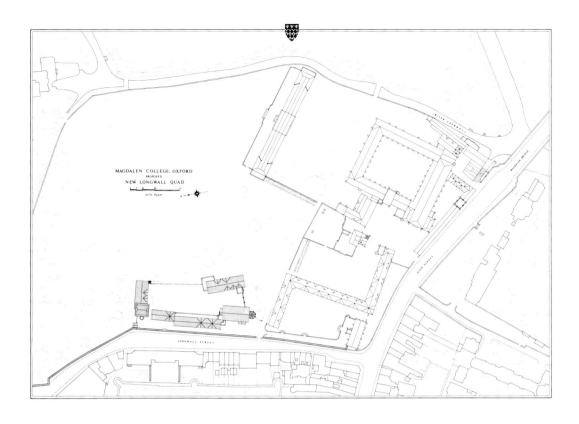

ABOVE: SITE PLAN; *BELOW*: PERSPECTIVE VIEW OF QUADRANGLE

THE NEW SQUARE IN FRONT OF NOTRE DAME CATHEDRAL; *OPPOSITE*: SITE PLAN OF COMPETITION PROJECT; *OVERLEAF*: THE NEW ST GERMAIN DISTRICT

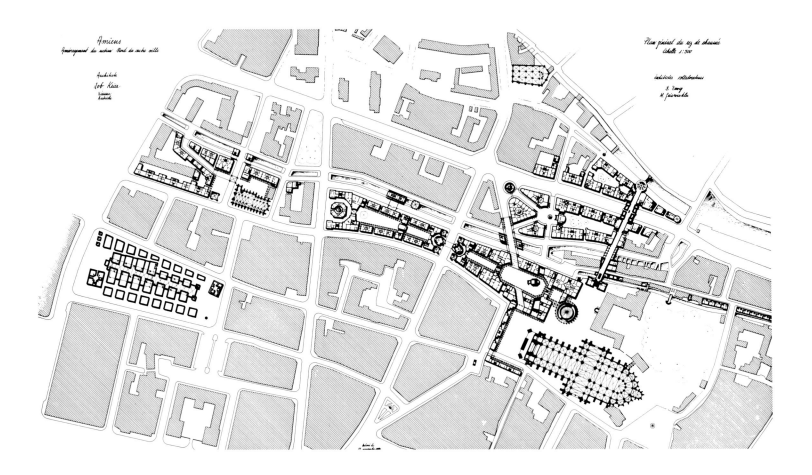

ROB KRIER
THE RECONSTRUCTION OF AMIENS
1984-91

' . . . Dites que vous allez à Bayreuth entendre un opéra de Wagner, à Amsterdam visiter une exposition de Primitifs flamands, on regrettera de ne pouvoir vous accompagner. Mais si vous avouez que vous allez voir, à la Pointe du Raz, une tempête, en Normandie, les pommiers en fleurs, à Amiens, une statue aimée de Ruskin, on ne pourra s'empêcher de sourire. Je n'en espère pas moins que vous irez à Amiens après m'avoir lu. . . ' Marcel Proust, 1900

The initial idea of the plan is simple: to erase the memory of war-time destruction by creating a new urban tissue similar to the original one and in the same location.

Three main points serve this basic assumption: the scale of the old city, the relationship of its public spaces, the traditional typology of the local buildings and their combination. These ideas were Krier's response to the competition launched by the city of Amiens in 1984.

His neighbourhood project is exact enough in its form, its definition of public space and its style to fulfil the requirements of such an urban programme, without altering the initial economy of the project.

Unlike a purely architectural plan dealing with quantity alone, the Krier plan includes the related architectural and urbanistic disciplines.

Creation of the South-North Axis – Linking the Parvis to the Saint-Leu Neighbourhood
The first part of the project deals with the wasteland that at present stretches between the Cathedral and what remains of the Saint-Leu neighbourhood.

The architect conceived of an urban tissue structured with very dense streets and squares linking the parvis to the bas parvis and the northern neighbourhood.

This junction includes a new pedestrian zone linking the Ancien Evêché south of the city to the rue d'Engoulvent north of the city by a succession of bridges with shops and cafes, similar to the Ponte Vecchio in Florence, above the streets and canals.

The University buildings planned for in the competition are laid out near the Cathedral at the meeting point of three squares: Notre-Dame square, the Ancien Evêché square and a newly built square halfway between the parvis and the canals: the Bas Parvis square.

The area includes the usual variety of shops found beside a religious monument, hotels, restaurants, bars, souvenir shops and other tourist attractions.

The East-West Axis – Relation Between the Parvis, Saint-Germain Neighbourhood and the Market Square
The plan provides the market with a major building: a glass enclosed gallery that runs through the covered market up to the belfry, surrounded by pavilions. The cellars of the market will be turned into an underground car park.

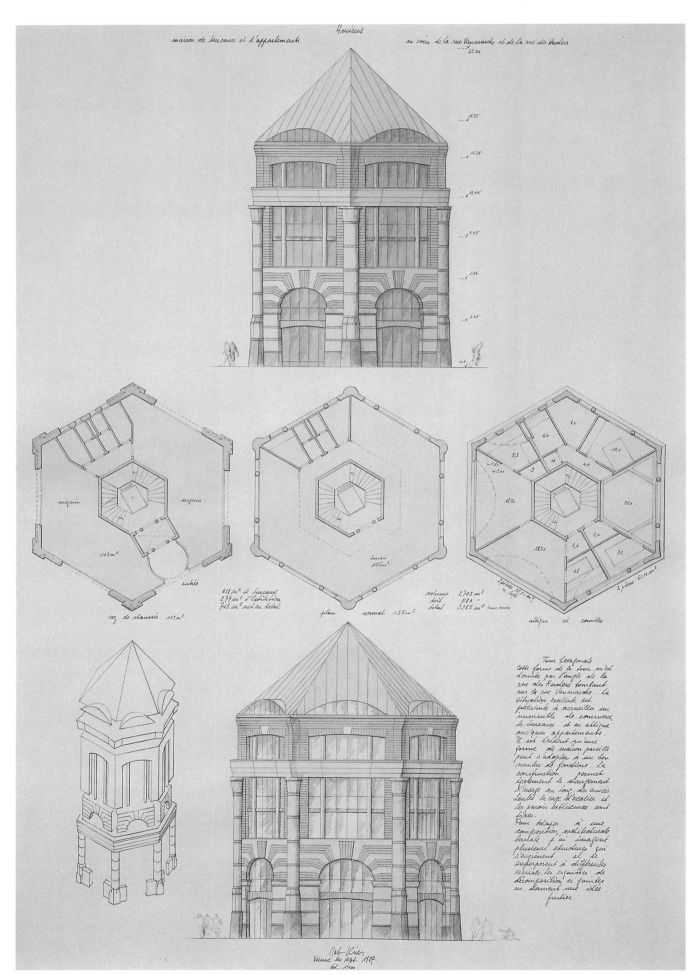

AN ADMINISTRATIVE BUILDING ON THE RUE VAN MARCKE

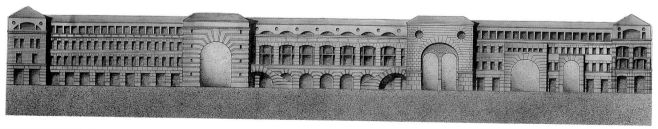

ABOVE LEFT AND RIGHT: THE UNIVERSITY AND ST LEU DISTRICT; THE SQUARE NAMED AFTER THE POET EDOUARD DAVID; *CENTRE LEFT AND RIGHT*: GOLDSMITHS' DISTRICT; THE PONTE VECCHIO

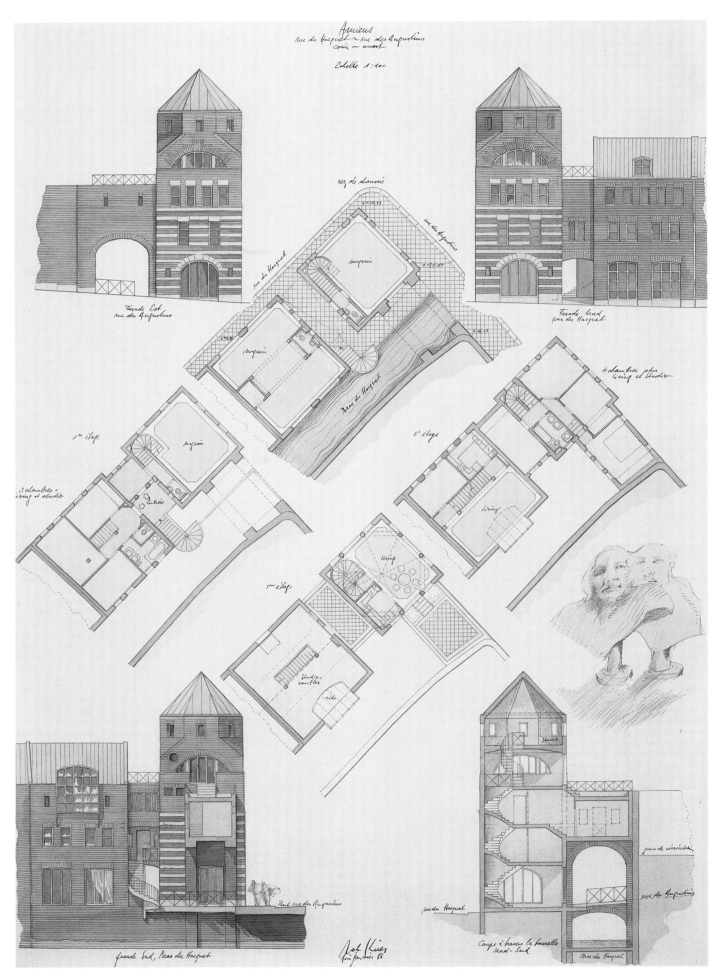

STUDY OF A HOUSE AT THE CORNER OF THE RUE DU HOCQUET AND RUE DES AUGUSTINS

64

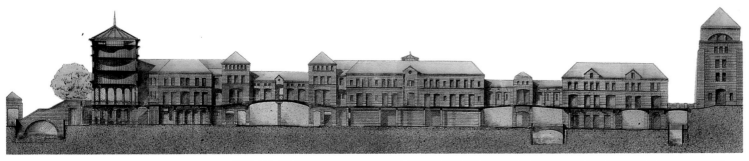

ABOVE LEFT AND RIGHT: THE NEW MARKET HALL INTEGRATED WITH EXISTING MARKET HALL, THE BELFRY AND CHURCH OF ST GERMAIN; THE CATHEDRAL SEEN FROM THE UNIVERSITY CAMPUS; *CENTRE LEFT AND RIGHT*: THE SQUARE IN FRONT OF THE CHURCH OF ST GERMAIN AND THE BELFRY; HOUSING ON AND ABOVE THE BRAS DES TANNEURS; HOUSES ON THE CANAL

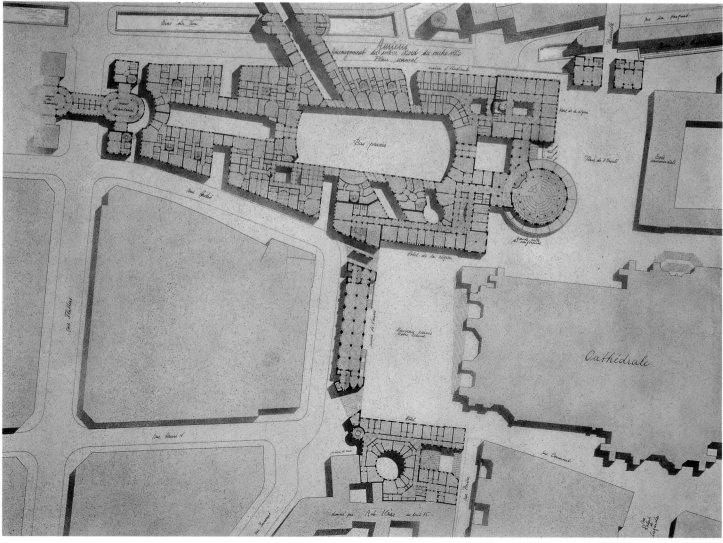

OPPOSITE: HOTEL ON THE CATHEDRAL SQUARE, AMIENS, 1989; *ABOVE*: COMPOSITION OF THE FACADE; *BELOW*: THE CATHEDRAL SQUARE WITH HOTEL AND UNIVERSITY CAMPUS

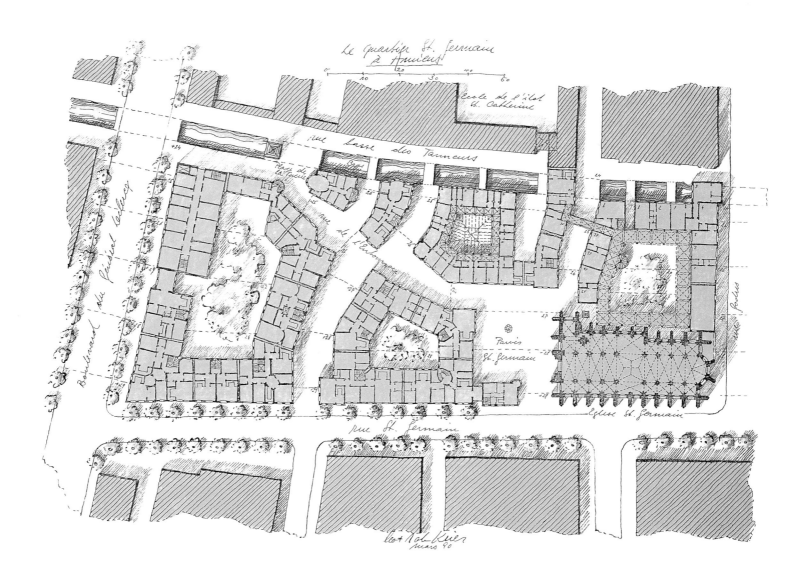

ABOVE: THE NEW ST GERMAIN DISTRICT; *BELOW*: 1:100 MODEL OF THE DISTRICT BUILT BY KRIER'S STUDENTS

In the Saint-Germain neighbourhood, a parvis is to be built in front of the church, and a new street will link the parvis diagonally to the canals. An inner pedestrian zone runs through the block formed by the rue Haute des Tanneurs and the rue des Orfèvres.

A small monument at each end – a pavilion in the rue du Marché Lanselles and a portico house in the rue Flatters – emphasises the new urban outline and street junctions.

Towards the canal, several buildings extend to the Bras des Tanneurs, some of them built over it in large arches. These picturesque fragments evoke the pre-war years, and give the impression of archeological layers, characteristic of the growth of the city.

The architects and engineers who undertook the post-war reconstruction of Amiens showed little concern for the historical plan of the city. They did not realise that they were thus depriving it of scale and character.

The Parvis of the Cathedral

The plan redefines the scale of Notre-Dame square by bringing it back to its medieval dimensions, thus emphasising the homogeneity of the cathedral created by the unique circumstance that all the statuary was produced by a single workshop.

This solution is similar to the present situation of Strasbourg Cathedral, one of the few cathedrals unaffected by 19th century urban renewal.

Urban Functions

Krier's project mingles all activities within the urban structure (shops, workshops, offices, university departments, cultural centres, etc) and pays particular attention to lodgings, indispensable to the creation of a lively centre.

One of the first steps in the study was to settle on the structure of public spaces and the scale of construction, an aim reached after a typological study of the buildings in the general plan.

Later on, an in-depth study of architectural styles (past and present) will help to build the new face of Amiens.

Trees

At present, very few streets in Amiens are planted with trees, and their width in relation to building heights creates a gloomy impression.

Krier proposes to create new alignments of trees and to fill inner courtyards with trees and plants.

The area will never recapture the picturesque charm one is able to see and that is suggested in old photographs, and the landscaping will thus make up for this.

Traffic and Car Park

The project maintains the plan of the existing streets, except for the rue Vanmarcke which is slightly corrected to keep a small triangular block of lodgings near the water edge.

All the streets can be reached by car, which avoids transforming a few streets into motorways.

Six hundred parking places are to be built underground, including 320 for the local residents. Each house has a garage while the other parking places are to be for both tourists and commuters.

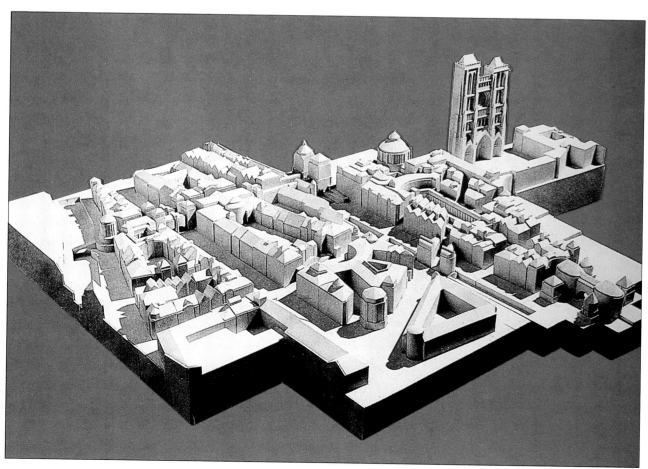

MODEL SHOWING THE AREA AROUND THE CATHEDRAL

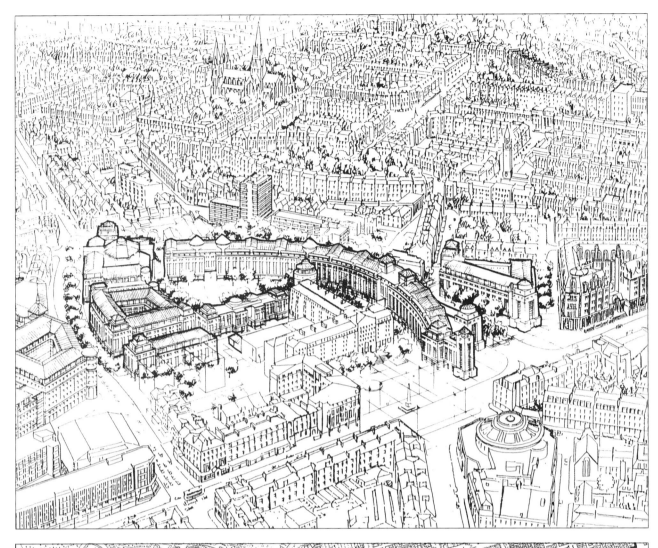

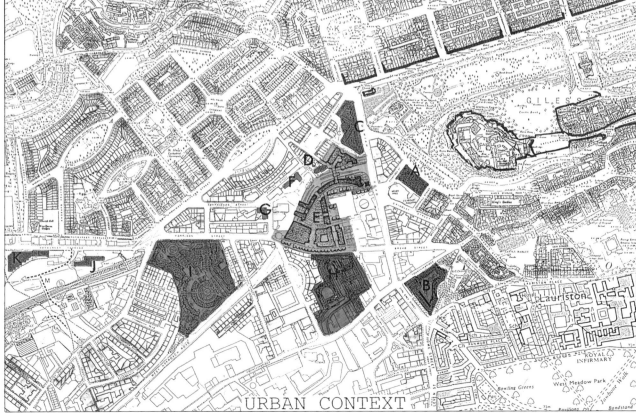

ABOVE: AERIAL VIEW; *BELOW:* PLAN SHOWING URBAN CONTEXT

TERRY FARRELL & COMPANY
EDINBURGH INTERNATIONAL CONFERENCE AND FINANCE CENTRE

Edinburgh has seen the development of three new towns in its history. This development, potentially a 'Fourth New Town', is sited at the west end of Princes Street in front of Edinburgh Castle, and contributes to important city views.

The Masterplan provides a new conference and exhibition centre for the City as well as a new office business centre, public parking and improvements to the environment of the existing hotels situated in the adjacent area. The plan uses the steeply sloping site to establish a mid-level public square,

fronting this with an office crescent and the conference centre.

Bulk, scale and height were recognised as important urban design considerations from the outset and several stages of public consultation were undertaken leading up to the eventual planning consent.

The scheme heals and repairs the area which was previously a railway goods yard. It utilises the new road approach to create a gateway to Edinburgh and improves the setting of the existing festival square.

ABOVE: SITE PLAN; *BELOW*: AERIAL PHOTOGRAPH SHOWING THE SITE OF THE FUTURE DEVELOPMENT

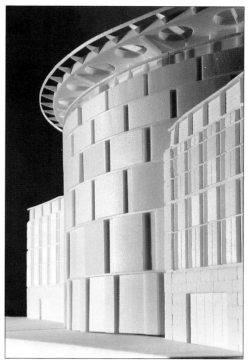

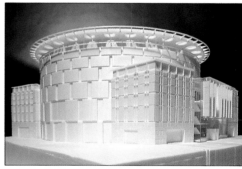

LEFT: View of the model; ABOVE: General and detail view of the conference centre; OVERLEAF: Aerial perspective

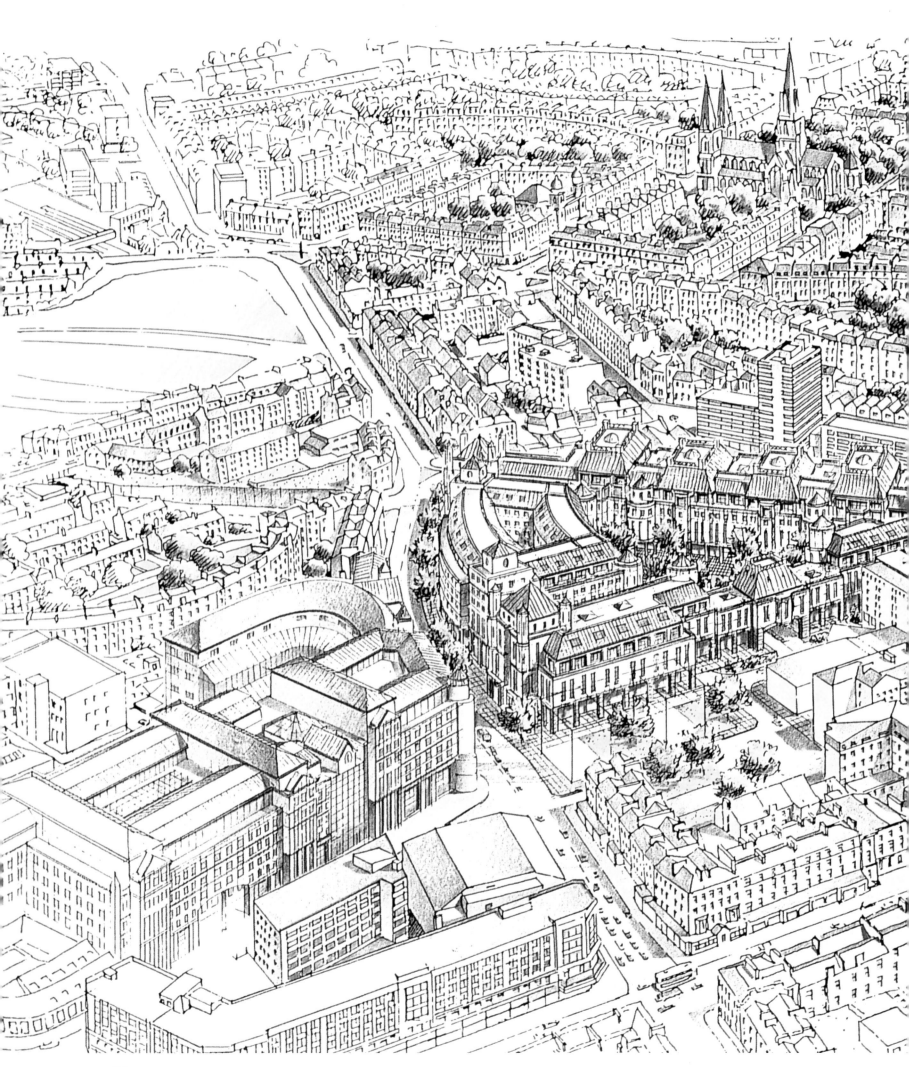

74

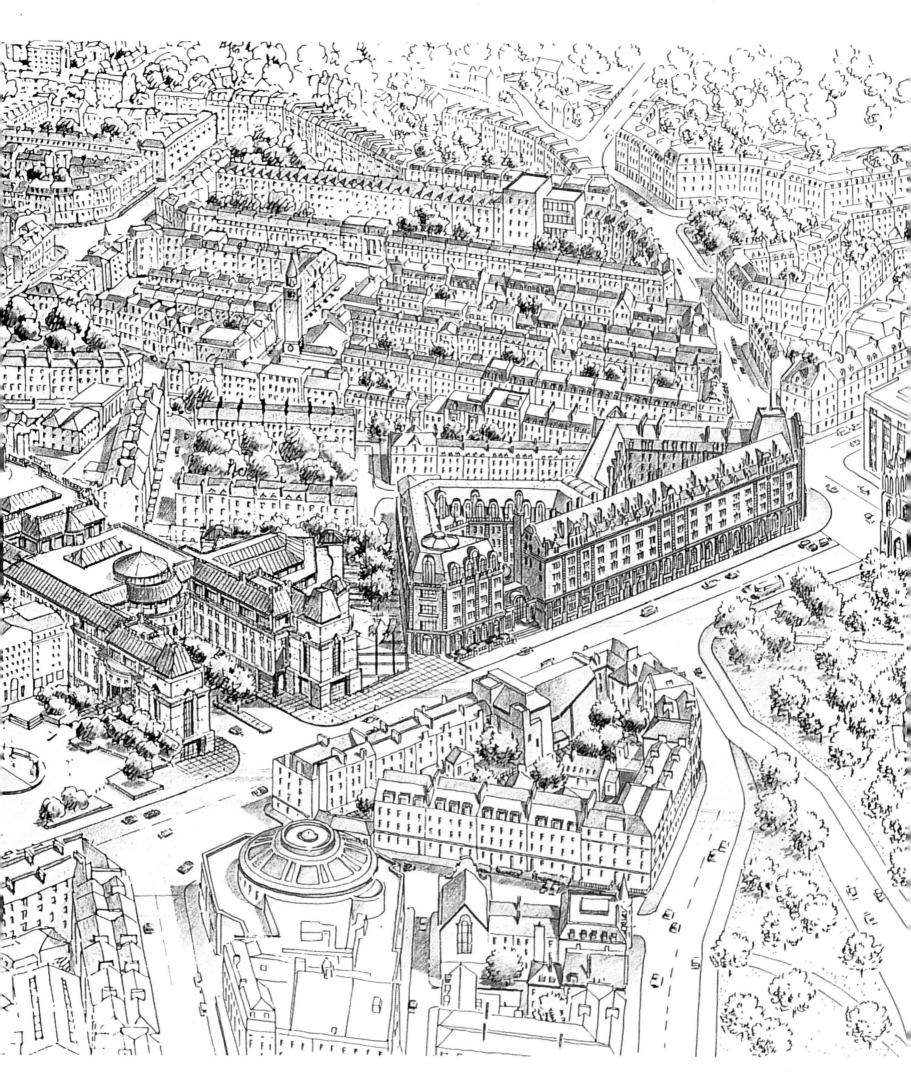

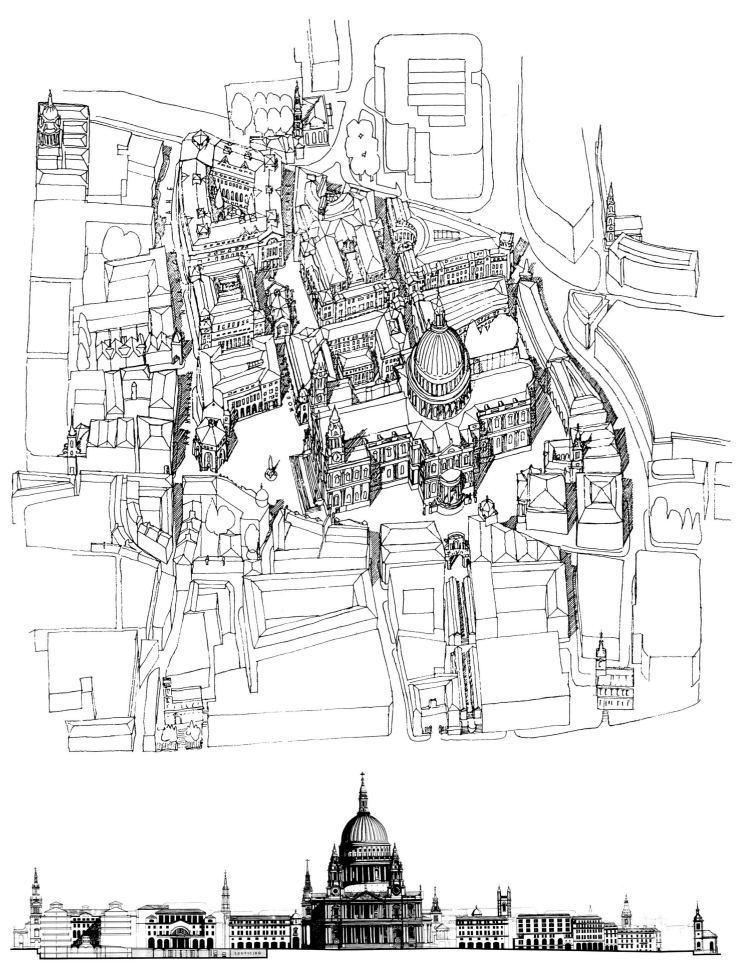

ABOVE: MASTERPLAN FOR THE REDEVELOPMENT OF THE BUILDINGS SURROUNDING ST PAUL'S; *BELOW*: SECTION ACROSS STREET FROM NEWGATE TO QUEEN VICTORIA STREET
SHOWING THE HEIGHT OF THE BLOCKS IN RELATION TO THE CATHEDRAL AND WREN'S STEEPLES AND CHURCH TOWERS; *OPPOSITE*: MASTERPLAN MODEL FOR THE ST PAUL'S AREA

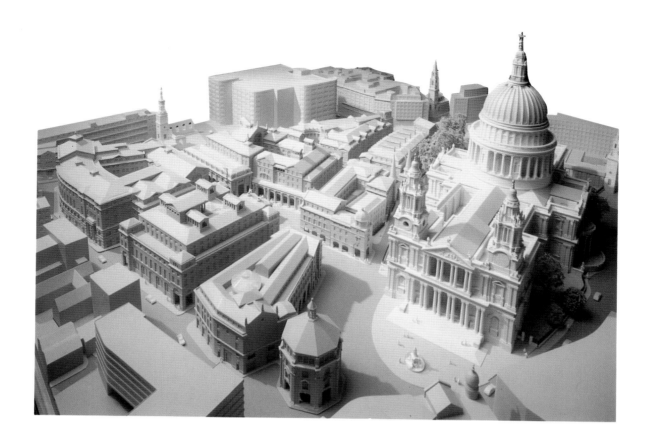

JOHN SIMPSON & PARTNERS
THE RECONSTRUCTION OF
THE AREA AROUND ST PAUL'S CATHEDRAL IN THE CITY OF LONDON

Until its destruction during the War, the St Paul's area worked as one homogenous whole. Over the centuries redevelopment had occurred but always on a piecemeal basis along the existing medieval street pattern, retaining the character of the area and a consistent relationship with the Cathedral. Following the war many plans were proposed but in spite of the long deliberations, particularly surrounding the Holford Plan, a consistent approach to the redevelopment has never been achieved.

In the early 1950s the area to the east and south-east of St Paul's Church Yard was cleared as part of a plan that proposed removing all the buildings within the immediate vicinity of St Paul's so that the Cathedral could be seen standing alone in the middle of open green space. While this was going on there was a change of approach and in the 1960s the area to the north was redeveloped according to the Holford plan. This bleak modernist style mega-structure, typical of the 1960s, quite deliberately obliterated the old street pattern and broke the urban continuity between St Paul's and the City to the north. To the south-west of the Cathedral is an enclave that survived the war and demolition under subsequent plans. In 1980 it was designated a conservation area although it is a little compromised by the heavy traffic along St Paul's Church Yard.

The result today is that the great Cathedral, rather than being at the centre of a lively and thriving urban quarter, lies at the edge of a series of developments of very different character in a sort of no mans land; its urban connections

physically severed from the rest of the City of London.

A limited architectural competition was held in 1985 for a design to redevelop the Holford area north of the Cathedral. It was limited to the northern side of St Paul's Cathedral and resulted in a series of designs that were just as inappropriate as the present buildings. It was after this that I prepared a counter scheme which proposed a masterplan for the whole St Paul's quarter. The aims were – firstly to emphasise the necessity for an overall consistent approach covering the whole area surrounding the Cathedral, essential if the post-war experience is not to be repeated; secondly, to propose that here of all places, next to St Paul's a monument of major architectural and historic importance, the case for a traditional approach must surely be overwhelming and thirdly, to demonstrate that a traditional approach to the planning and architecture of the area can satisfy contemporary commercial, functional and technical criteria.

The masterplan used the surviving area to the south-west of the Cathedral as a model. Walking within this conservation area you get a glimpse of what the whole of the St Paul's area might have been like before its destruction. It is typical of the City of London which is built upon a medieval street pattern. This pattern, apart from pockets such as Paternoster Square, has survived fairly well despite repeated rebuilding over the years and it is this that has given the City its special character which has survived from one generation of buildings to the next.

The City is thus characterised by a network of fairly narrow

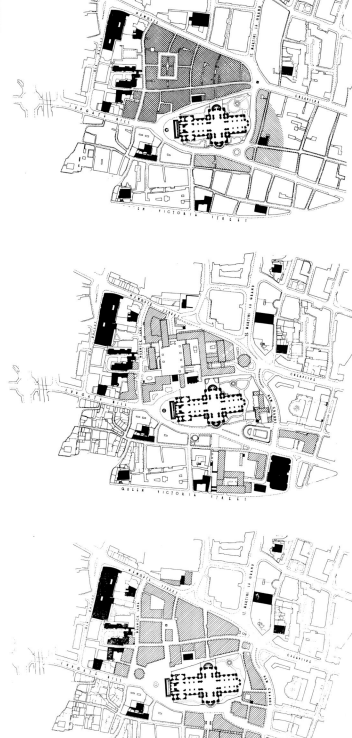

LEFT: Painting by Carl Laubin of Paternoster Square showing how the dome of the Cathedral would dominate; ABOVE: Pre-war plan of the St Paul's area before bombing; CENTRE: Plan showing area today as it is after the redevelopment (heavily hatched buildings are listed, lightly hatched are the most offensive of the post-war blocks); BELOW: The Masterplan (hatched buildings indicate the extent of the proposals)

MODEL OF MASTERPLAN FOR THE ST PAUL'S AREA VIEWED FROM THE EAST

streets and lanes that follow an irregular pattern. Monuments, church towers and steeples serve the function of providing orientation within this tight labyrinth of streets. Views of these landmarks are revealed gradually on the skyline or at the end of a winding street or alleyway. The buildings along these streets are tightly packed, and blocks are usually built up of a series of terraced buildings ranging in general from between four to eight-storeys high. Public space has traditionally been at a premium and in general big open squares within the City are very rare indeed. Where they do occur, they are generally hard paved. On the rare occasion where one does come across green open space as in St Paul's Church Yard or Ireland Yard it is distinctly defined by iron railings.

Even around the Cathedral space is tight so, without the benefit of a grand forecourt or an axial approach, St Paul's was designed to dominate through the sheer contrast between the grandeur of its architecture and the small-scale informality of its immediate neighbours – rather in the manner of a Gothic cathedral surrounded by a closely packed irregular collection of small domestic buildings.

Wren's design for the Cathedral is therefore very much the product of its 'Gothic' type setting. Rather than the giant order preferred in his Great Model, in the built version he uses two stacked orders endowing the building with detail of a smaller scale and more intricate nature.

The dome too is lifted up onto a drum and the building is generally designed to be appreciated at close quarters. It is not designed as most Baroque buildings to make an impact and be seen along a great vista. Instead, the height of the base of the upper order is arranged so as to start just a little higher than the roof of the surrounding buildings (about four-storeys high) thus creating the illusion of the great Cathedral hovering on the skyline over the roofs of its surrounding buildings. It is one of those great designs that is best appreciated within its setting

rather than in splendid isolation.

In order to do justice to Christopher Wren's design and recreate the urban character of the surrounding area it is quite clear that it is essential to reintroduce the old medieval street pattern and through this re-establish the old relationship between the Cathedral and its surroundings and make it once again an integral part of the City of London.

Thus the masterplan re-establishes the old building lines where possible. Around the Cathedral churchyard to the north the Chapter House is restored within a street facade and to the south the open sites are filled in to continue the old street line. The south-west corner is tightened where the churchyard leaks out hopelessly into Cannon Street and where the old street pattern is obliterated by the addition of New Change. The choir school is replaced by four new urban blocks that firmly enclose the Cathedral on the east. At the west front of St Paul's a new Cathedral Square is created that is intentionally larger than its pre-war predecessor.

The main streets beyond the churchyard such as Paternoster Row to the north and Carter Lane to the south are reinstated connecting back to the surrounding streets. Paternoster Row for instance continues the line of Cheapside linking the City's main shopping street into the St Paul's area and brings commercial activity into the very heart of the quarter. Along the length of both these streets narrow roads and lanes reveal dramatic views of the Cathedral similar to those for which the area was historically renowned – the view from Dean's Court being a typical example.

Opposite the south transept Peters steps, which lead down to the River Thames, have been kept even though they were only introduced since the war. They have however been narrowed down with a colonnade and shops either side to make them more characteristic of the area. Temple Bar, an arched gateway attributed to Wren and designed to go across the Fleet

VIEW OF CURRENT MODEL OF AREA NORTH OF THE CATHEDRAL LOOKING ALONG PATERNOSTER ROW TOWARDS THE NEW SQUARE

Street entrance to the City but removed in the 19th century, is repositioned as a gateway at the head of the steps. This route would be the approach used by tourists arriving to see St Paul's by coach. They would come in off Queen Victoria Street to the south allowing St Paul's Church Yard to be cleared of unsightly coach parking.

Inevitably, the height, size and bulk of the buildings is a crucial aspect of the masterplan. In the immediate vicinity of St Paul's the buildings need to be of a small enough scale to relate to Wren's design and are designed to be of a similar type to those surviving buildings to the south-west of St Paul's Church Yard. Moving away from the Cathedral however, it is desirable in order to achieve a gradual transition across the area to increase the size of the blocks on the periphery to correspond to those of post-war London, Bracken House for example. As London buildings have grown somewhat since the days when Wren designed St Paul's and his City churches, for a successful city townscape to be created it has been essential to ensure that these public buildings and monuments continue to stand out and dominate the new private ones despite an increase in size.

The masterplan is designed to create an urban quarter in the traditional sense that restores the setting for St Paul's Cathedral and the other surviving monuments and buildings. It does this by redesigning the new blocks to respond to contemporary commercial and functional requirements in terms of depth and size but also to relate to the old London street pattern and the traditional hierarchy between public and private buildings.

In 1987 the Prince of Wales drew attention to the St Paul's area with his now famous Mansion House speech. In 1990 the new owners of the Paternoster Square site north of St Paul's responded to the Prince's challenge and took up this masterplan which has since been developed in detail along the northern side of the churchyard.

Inevitably because of additional constraints such as lease restrictions, covenants, ownership boundaries and the outcome of negotiations between various landowners, the location and positions of blocks within the plan required adjustment. The new Paternoster Square was moved further east in order to exclude Sudbury House, the block at the north-west corner of the site, as it was not within the same ownership.

Once the masterplan was firmed up eight architects were commissioned to design individual buildings. Before they began their designs they were provided with a series of criteria that determined the height and size of the building, cornice lines, set backs and so on as well as the kind of building prototype envisaged on their site. The architects responded to this in different ways to bring in a variety of architecture but within the spirit of the masterplan. Planning permission has been granted by the City of London Corporation for these buildings together with the design for the new Sudbury House. This site, although small in the context of the overall quarter around St Paul's, is crucial to the masterplan for the area. It contains Paternoster Square, the second largest public space after St Paul's Church Yard, but most importantly contains the only mega structure in the immediate vicinity of the Cathedral and cannot be developed on a piecemeal basis. All the other buildings surrounding St Paul's are independent blocks that can be redeveloped separately by their individual owners on a block by block basis in the orthodox manner.

By replacing this mega structure with a series of traditional urban blocks the way is clear for a consistent redevelopment plan to be applied all around the Cathedral.

In this respect the Paternoster Square scheme may be only the first phase in a long process but it is absolutely critical in opening the way for the complete rehabilitation of St Paul's Cathedral within a traditional urban framework and as an integral part of the City of London.

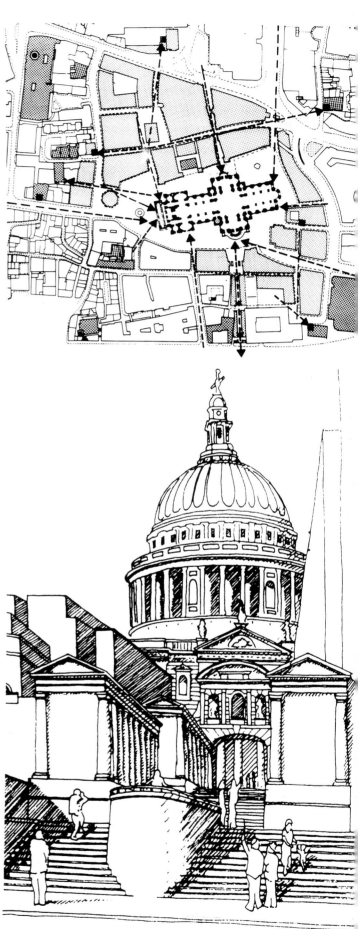

LEFT: Painting by Carl Laubin of the square at the west front of the Cathedral; ABOVE: Plan showing views and vistas which are used to maintain a hierarchy between the public and private buildings; BELOW: View looking up Peters steps towards the south transept

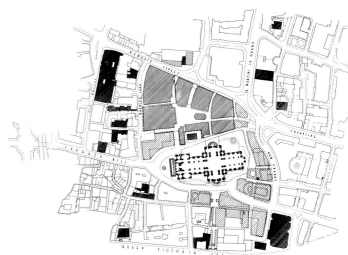

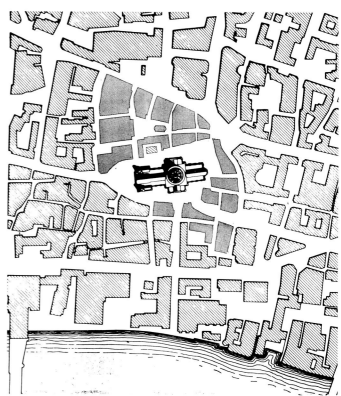

LEFT: *The Current Masterplan (showing the Market Building by John Simpson & Partners); ABOVE: Plan of the Current Masterplan; BELOW: The Current Masterplan in context*

85

FACADE OF ONE OF THE BUILDINGS TO BE RECONSTRUCTED (LOT 3: PROJECT BY S ASSASSIN, B DUMONS, P GISCLARD, N PRAT), RUE DE LAEKEN, BRUSSELS

MAURICE CULOT

A STREET !

The Reconstruction of the Rue de Laeken, Brussels

The AG group – a Belgian insurance company – and the Fondation pour l'Architecture in Brussels launched a Europe-wide consultation, aimed at young architects, for the reconstruction of a row of 15 houses in one of Brussels' oldest streets: the rue de Laeken.

The reconstruction operation, scheduled to be completed by spring 1992, had a double objective: firstly, to demonstrate the aesthetic, functional and economic value of the traditional plot terrain in the construction of quality housing in a historic city centre; and secondly, to discover and launch young architects from the European Community who had chosen to work on the restoration of historic centres.

Planning and co-ordination of the work started in early 1990 by The Atelier d'Architecture Atlante. Maurice Culot, architect and urbanist, is President of the Fondation pour l'Architecture.

In the moments before I start writing a text, all the different ways of broaching the subject-matter run through my mind like the permutations of fruits and bells on a one-armed bandit. With some prompting from my subconscious, I came upon a possible introduction to this piece which appears as forceful as it is concise: 'A street, Ladies and Gentlemen! A street!'

Think of the money, energy and organisation behind an architectural competition aimed at the finest young architects in Europe. Think of the effort required to achieve the reconstruction of a few terrace houses – a fragment – let alone a whole street like this! More streets were created in the still much-maligned 19th century than in all of the previous ones put together, but that is history. In the first half of this century architects came to wish for the death of the street, despite their supposed knowledge of the city. At the beginning of the 1920s, one of the best known of these architects unhesitatingly compared the street with a 'dusty corridor'. This was enough to ignite a flame which in no time at all had the ability to make a street go up in smoke.

Even though it is obsessed with communication, our era is incapable of producing a street – a place of constant exchange in different cultures and societies throughout history. In the past few years, a growing awareness of the environment has once again focused attention on the traditional town – although agreement has still to be reached on what exactly this means, for the concept of the town is as abused as that of the street. According to the standard French dictionary, a town is 'a geographical and social environment formed by an organic and relatively large-scale grouping of structures, whose inhabitants work, for the most part, within the agglomeration; in business, industry or administration'.

Ill-defined though it may be, the recovery of the town has become not only desirable but also essential. This is now recognised by many people, including investors, as the competition

proves. To continue maintaining that current sociological and economic conditions are not conducive to such reconstruction is as foolhardy as believing that the economy is powered solely by production. As Michel Henochsberg observed: 'Innovations and initiatives form the life-blood which animates and inspires a sphere of production that is much more consequent than causal.' [1]

The same reasoning lies behind the cultural and financial commitment to the rue de Laeken project, which does not stop with the reconstruction of the street itself but attempts to define a framework for similar projects. So there was good cause for broadening the scope of consultation to architects throughout Europe. On the one hand, the problem is a European one; although the accent may vary, the situation in Brussels is paralleled everywhere else. On the other hand, given the loss of our urban-planning skills, it makes sense to draw into the project as many of those as possible who want to see the reconstruction of the city and who are not prisoners of the dominant system of architectural production. This means mostly young people. However, this should not be seen as an act of discrimination but rather as a part of a recovery strategy that is making an appeal to fresh forces. I hope this reassures those older than 40, whose advice and comments are the natural and indispensable complement to the work in progress.

The jury had the double satisfaction of unanimously selecting the prize-winners and seeing the political authorities (who were present at its deliberations) recognise the pentagon defined by the inner boulevards as a Historic Centre. The beneficial effects of the reconstruction of the rue de Laeken on the surrounding neighbourhood will soon become apparent; clearly, the same kind of attention should be extended to the scarred and little-loved centre as a whole.

The improvement of the historic centre of the city in general presupposes a reversal of the behaviour that led to its neglect and a rehabilitation of procedures that were condemned and excluded by the narrow, puritanical code of modernism. This means that young architects may renew the practices of copying, imitation, reproduction, pastiche and borrowing, recognising that a sound general knowledge of architecture is the necessary basis for finding the most adequate solutions to the complex issues of reconstruction. The architects tackling the rue de Laeken competition had to simultaneously confront a number of problems, deciding how to:

— integrate new buildings into a run-down historic quarter.

— design street facades in harmony with existing ones, following mainly neo-classical conventions of ornament and composition.

— design rear facades overlooking a garden as well as prestige office buildings: the traditional Brussels solution of composing these without regard for aesthetic considerations was unpermissible.

— define a typology which incorporated these basic ideas within

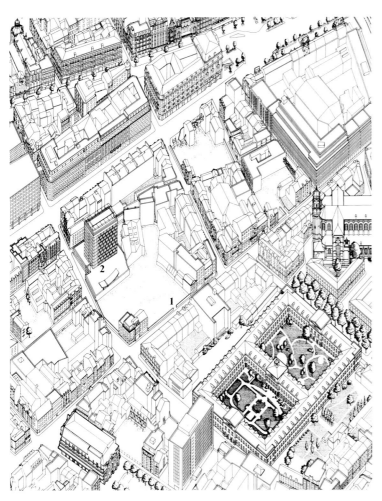

coherent plans and sections, also taking into account the relation with the common underground car park.

— satisfy contemporary living standards and equally exacting financial and technical constraints.

The operation is complex, that is the essence of its modernity. Its ultimate aim: to create the impression of a street which has always been there while at the same time give the feeling of renewal.

The competition and its outcome thus combine and take on a dynamic of their own. The difficulty lies in the combination of all the projects – the facades, plans and sections – into a coherent whole, not just a haphazard juxtaposition of individual intentions.

The competition should therefore be understood as a framework which binds together the different partners. The Fondation pour l'Architecture safeguards the design on behalf of the contestants and guarantees the validity of the project as a whole on behalf of the jury. The co-ordinating architect prepares the single application for a building permit and where necessary suggests modifications to the prize-winners. The investor is responsible for the smooth running of the project and ultimately for the quality of the reconstruction, which is widely expected to serve as something of a manifesto throughout its different stages, from the competition itself to the inauguration of the buildings in 1992.

A two-year wait is a short time in the life of a town, but a long time in ours. I shall try to alleviate your impatience by revealing how you too can make use of this work, which can simply be a trigger for your imagination. Let us concentrate, for example, on the facades. Close your eyes with me. I see faces – facade-faces. Here, some elements have been emphasised, a shadow accentu-

ABOVE LEFT: DETAIL OF AXONOMETRIC PLAN OF BRUSSELS SHOWING: 1 THE COMPETITION SITE; 2 THE AG HIGH-RISE TO BE REPLACED WITH A BUILDING THAT

ated, a beauty spot added in the form of a false window. In our society, it is only hypocrisy which makes life bearable; lying can get us out of the worst situations, while make-up can give us a hundred different faces. If our eyes are satisfied, our imagination is stimulated. Making architecture seductive is decidedly more civil and urbane than insisting that it be truthful. For what happens if this truthful architecture is detestable? I predict that the only future left for the town is to be a theatre – and not simply because I like to raise all problems to the level of paradox. One could see the apartments as boxes, the facades as backdrops and the squares and streets as both stage and auditorium.

— But you are confusing life with fiction.
— In these uncertain times, this does not displease me.
— You advocate artifice over the bare-faced concrete?
— Of course!
— The amoral over the moral?
— Definitely.
— But is that good mannered?
— Let's just call it 'mannered'.

Let us counter progress with artfulness and allow ourselves to be seduced by the projects for the reconstruction of the rue de Laeken, which promise to provide a superb inhabited backdrop. As for the play, we can wager that the people of Brussels will know how it should be done.

Notes

1   Michel Henochsberg, 'L'économie victorienne', in *Libération*, 12 February 1990.

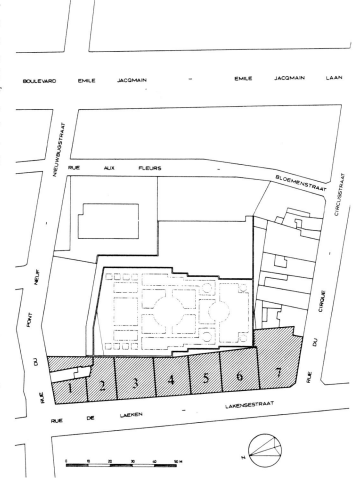

LINE; *BELOW*: ELEVATION SHOWING STREET AS IT WILL APPEAR AFTER ITS COMPLETION IN 1993; *ABOVE RIGHT*: SITE PLAN SHOWING COMPETITION LOTS 1 TO 7

Gabriele Tagliaventi and *Marco Gaiani* have focused their research on the study of urban models and classical and vernacular architecture. The project testifies to their ability to treat the street as a whole, while absorbing the context and scale of this very distinctive quarter of Brussels. Gaiani and Tagliaventi made their two buildings fit unostentatiously into the street. This valid perception of the urban scale stood out more than the details of the projects and plans themselves.

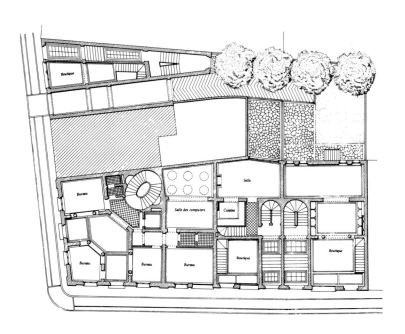

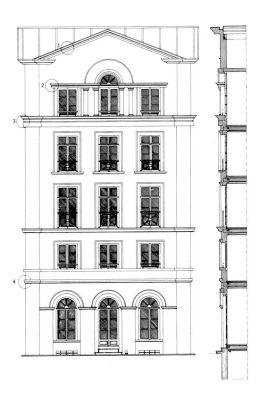

Atelier 55 skilfully interpret the characteristics of neo-classical architecture to take account of the requirements of the brief with their scheme. This interpretation unselfconsciously assimilates the eclectic and neo-rationalist tendencies of the last century, revealing a profound knowledge of the distinctive features of the architecture in the centre of Brussels. This clearly contributes to the success of the street facade although the rear is dissipated by a surfeit of compositional elements.

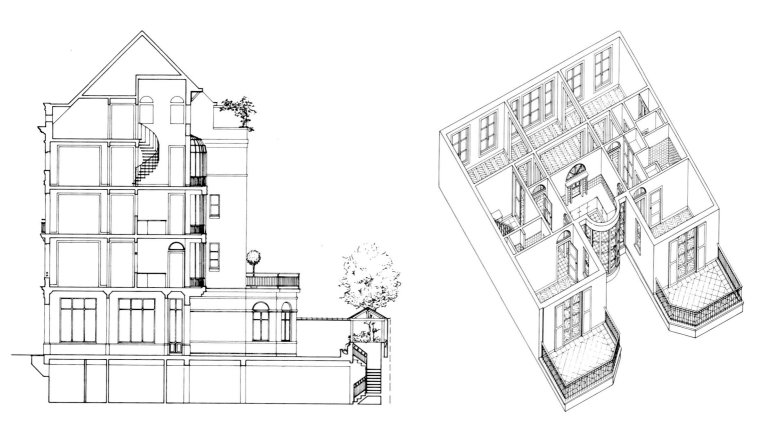

Sylvie Assassin, *Bathelemy Dumons*, *Philippe Gisclard* and *Nathalie Prat* *produced a scheme which won the unanimous approval of the jury. In both the street and garden facades and the plans, the composition of the buildings bears witness to the architects' assured and inventive approach towards typology – an approach maintained consistently through each of the schemes. The team are concerned with the promotion of traditional architecture through building and other methods.*

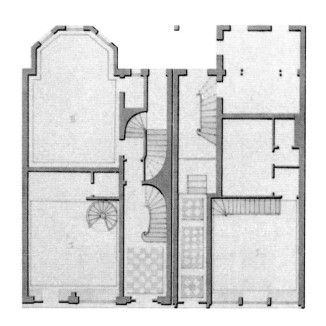

Jean-Philippe Garric and *Valérie Nègre* were deemed by several members of the jury to have created one of the most beautiful schemes submitted to them. It represents classical intervention on a grand scale. The sections are ingeniously organised; the public and communal spaces are excellently thought out. The accord between the project and its presentation reflects the philosophy that the two disciplines of architecture and drawing are interlinked and mutually supportive.

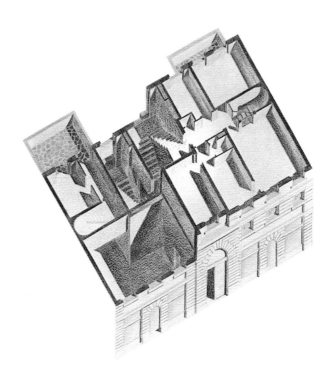

Javier Cenicacelaya and *Inigo Salona* have responded to the brief with a scheme which, while extremely precise, still conveys their own brand of artistic expression, rooted in their Basque culture. The clarity of the facades and plans expresses their desire for realism and rationality, the distribution of internal spaces reveals their concern for the quality of housing. The different spaces are clearly hierarchical and articulated and there is a diversity in the visual sequence.

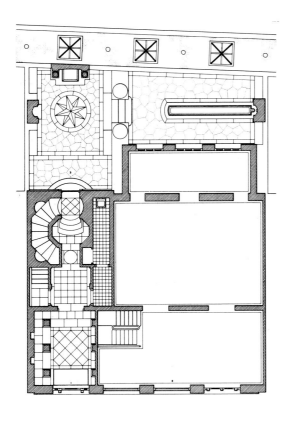

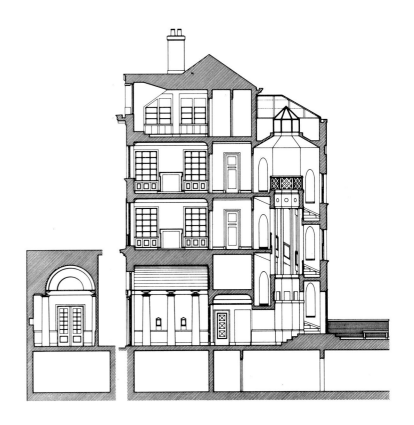

Liam O'Connor and *John Robins* propose to extend the building-line of the terrace to the very end of the rue de Laeken. A similar arrangement had previously been used in the construction of new quarters. It allows the creation of a small internal public space around which the housing and architects' studios are organised. There was however an unfortunate decision about the position of a car parking ramp which the jury felt favoured the car over the comfort of the pedestrian.

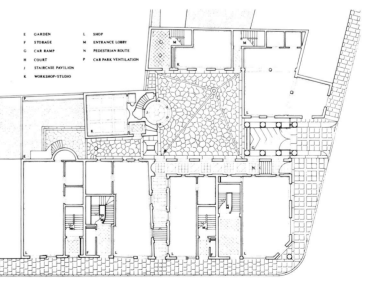

E   GARDEN   L   SHOP

F   STORAGE   M   ENTRANCE LOBBY

G   CAR RAMP   N   PEDESTRIAN ROUTE

H   COURT   P   CAR PARK VENTILATION

J   STAIRCASE PAVILION

K   WORKSHOP·STUDIO

Joseph Altuna and *Marie-Laure Petit* *produced a scheme of great simplicity which deploys the most original composition. The essential source of inspiration is the site itself. The* modus operandi *is imitation, the architects follow the same principles that underpinned the renovation of the street at the beginning of the 19th century. This approach is evident in the treatment of the corner building where the first floor windows emulate those on some of the finest of the street's facades.*

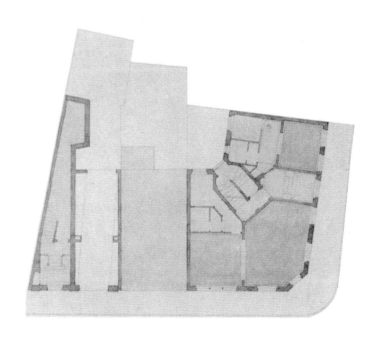